MARXISM AND THE CLASS STRUGGLE

Contents

I	From philosophy to the class struggle	1
II	The materialist conception of history: part one	28
III	The materialist conception of history: part two	52
IV	Classes and class struggle: the economic base	72
V	Classes and class struggle: politics and revolution	95
VI	Ideology and political economy in Marx's *Capital*	128
VII	Marxist theory and class consciousness	151
	Select bibliography	165

Foreword

The studies collected in this volume do not pretend to be a comprehensive survey of the theories of Marx. They are but an elementary statement of the place of Marx's concepts 'class' and 'class struggle' in his doctrine as a whole. For this reason, the only aim of the book is to encourage a thorough study of the writings of Marx and Engels, as well as, of course, Lenin and Trotsky and all those who were able to develop Marxism, understanding it to be 'a guide to action' in the proletarian revolution. Once this study of the original sources is undertaken, the emptiness and, in the main, gross ignorance, of the many fashionable 'commentaries' on Marxism is apparent.

Chapters II, III, IV and V, and part of Chapter I, were originally published in *Workers Press* in June-July 1971. The second part of Chapter I is to be found, except for minor modifications, in my pamphlet, *Lenin on Dialectics,* 1963. Chapters VI and VII were first published in the journal *Fourth International* for Winter 1971-72 and Summer 1974 respectively.

C. Slaughter
May 1975

I
From philosophy to the class struggle

> It is only in an order of things in which there are no more classes and class antagonisms that *social evolutions* will cease to be *political revolutions*. Till then, on the eve of every general reshuffling of society the last word of social science will always be: '*Le combat ou la mort, la lutte sanguinaire ou le néant. C'est ainsi que la question est invinciblement posée.*' ['Combat or death: bloody struggle or extinction. Thus the question is inexorably posed.'] — George Sand. (*The Poverty of Philosophy*, p. 147.)

Marxism and Sociology

Marxism was born in the second quarter of the 19th century, the period which also gave birth to 'sociology'. Marxism is not 'another sociology', but the opposite of sociology. Marx did not accept the idea of a general science of 'social facts' with its own sphere, separate from the theory of knowledge, the natural sciences and history. His theories were a practical critique of existing society, an effort to provide a 'conscious head' for those forces within existing society whose material conditions necessitated a struggle for its overthrow.

Sociology is essentially an acceptance of the 'facts' of social life, and the attempt to determine the regularities and laws of their connections. For the most part, sociologists reject any philosophical outlook, i.e., they do not consciously understand any coherence or order in the *concepts* with which they select, define, abstract and interrelate the 'facts'. The classification and ordering of these facts has been modelled, insofar as any conscious plan exists, on the methods of the natural sciences.

This search for an objectivity (absence of 'value-judgement') akin to that established by natural science arises from a view of 'social facts' as things entirely external to the observer and consciousness, and therefore capable of being predicted in their movement and pattern. However, every 'sociology', every summary of social experience in consciousness, is in turn itself a component of history and change. The sociologist's verdict enters the consciousness of social actors. It will strengthen the cohesion of a ruling group, or it will disrupt it, or it will awaken ruled, oppressed groups to an understanding of their oppression, or it will 'explain' the necessity of their oppression, etc. All this in addition to the fact that the existing consciousness of these classes enters the conceptual equipment of the sociologist in the first place and predetermines (according to its character) what he 'discovers'.

Marxists explain the 'necessity' of social relations as they are found, but Marxist theory considers this necessity as a relative equilibrium, which will at a certain stage be disrupted and surpassed through the maturing of a struggle of internal opposed forces in the society. The 'statistical' regularities of sociologists reflect repetitive processes and quantitative changes, and until they lead to qualitative changes, then statistical laws of the sociologist's type may serve as the basis of 'predictions' or explanations, in the same way as administrators and businessmen can forecast behaviour. All human behaviour is conscious, but the relationships between different persons, classes and sectors of their behaviour are not necessarily contained in their consciousness, and so there are changes, indeed decisive ones, which 'do not first pass through consciousness', as Lenin put it. ('What the "Friends of the People" are and How they help the Social Democrats', *Collected Works*, Volume I)

One of the tasks of the Marxist theory of society and history is to ascertain the relationship between conscious and unconscious processes in different stages of social development. For example the relation between revolution and consciousness is a vital question; but it would be a mistake to suppose a single, *general* relation between them: the *proletarian* revolution will not show the same relation between unconscious and conscious factors as has appeared in earlier revolutions.

The very historical appearance of Marxism, as of sociology, and their further development, are not just the chance products of 'mind' suddenly turning its attention to social theory, which we then critically appraise, judging right or wrong. On the contrary, the historical appearance and development of Marxism and sociology are specific expressions of consciousness in relation to the development of definite classes in definite surroundings, working over the previously acquired philosophical, historical, political, economic, aesthetic, ethical, etc., ideological heritage. It is not now a question of selecting this or that part of Marxism or of sociology and combining, comparing or contrasting them, but of placing them historically in relation to definite social forces, tracing the conflict and interpenetration of these forces and of the theories corresponding to them.

On this basis the person making the historical analysis must also consciously grasp his own role in the relations being analysed and the history of his own concepts. For Marx this is the only real objectivity — the conscious development of one's theory as the expression and instrument of a definite class in history.

We are already discussing an unbridgeable gap between Marxism as a world outlook and all 'sociologies' and 'philosophies'. Marxist method adopts the standpoint of thinking which enters the activity and movement of the working class in order to transform the social order through the dictatorship of the proletariat and conscious creation of a classless society:

> The standpoint of the old materialism is civil society; the standpoint of the new is human society, or socialized humanity. (*Theses on Feuerbach*. No. I, 1845.)

This 'socialized humanity' was potentially created by capitalism itself and must overthrow capitalism. Marxism came into existence as a result of 'overcoming' (*aufheben*) the contradictions reached in the evolution of existing philosophy, socialist theory and political economy: it overcame them by ending the separate existence of each, seeing them as definite forms of reflection of the social relations from which they sprang: in this synthesis (negation) they form the possibility of a new development. But that development is not in the sphere of independent thought. Thought must become the expression of the movement of that social force (the proletariat) which actively transforms the material conditions responsible for the existing contradictions in each sphere of life and thought.

Theory and practice now united. 'Revolutionary practice' overcame both the unconscious clash of material forces and the illusory independent play of thought. *Philosophy was 'realized in the proletariat'*. 'Just as philosophy finds its material weapons in the proletariat, so the proletariat finds its intellectual weapons in philosophy.' (Marx, *Critique of Hegel's Philosophy of Right*, 1844)

This *conscious* unity of theory and practice, through bringing them into conflict, is the core of Marxism, which distinguishes it from both vulgar or mechanical materialism and idealism. It also necessarily distinguishes it from all 'sociologies' or 'explanations' of the social system.

> The philosophers have only interpreted the world, in various ways; the point is to change it. (Marx, *Theses on Feuerbach*. No. XI, 1845)

Once these beginnings (in both the historical and the 'logical' sense) are forgotten or misunderstood, Marxism stands in danger of being distorted and turned into something of a quite different nature. Hence Marx's 'I am not a Marxist'. Similarly Engels warned in his later life against those who learned the 'basic elements' of the materialist conception of history and then 'applied' these to any and every historical situation. Instead they were required by the Marxist method to make an independent investigation of the actual development, to demonstrate the historical origins and destiny of the forces at work.

Marxism has been criticized for neglecting the historical role of human consciousness, while sociologists of various kinds claim in one way or another to take this 'factor' into account. The opposite is the truth. Marxism explains consciousness as the reflection of social existence, the essence of which is man's struggle against nature, the development of productive forces and social relations of production. But to have shown this origin of the content of thought is not thereby to have reduced it to a cipher, any more than the 'explanation' of the necessary conditions for any phenomenon thereby 'explains it away'. Thought is a *necessary* link in the chain, its actual role going through many different types of phases; it is not just a sort of shimmering halo dazzling the eyes of the historian and making difficult his view of the 'real' history.

When the bourgeois sociologist, however, makes his judgement on social 'regularities', he *assumes* that the consciousness of the participants will remain at the same level and will continue to produce the same type of result. An extreme example is Michels' *Iron Law of Oligarchy*. Michels assumes that his generalizations from the mentality of the masses in class-divided societies is a 'fact' of human nature which will always stand in the same relation to the phenomena called 'large-scale organizations'. Among the factors underlying his 'iron law', Michels lists: 'the political indifference of the masses', 'their need for guidance' and 'the gratitude felt by the crowd for those who lead and write on their behalf'. But the reality is, in fact, contradictory: the very repetition of certain typical acts produces situations where the acts *cannot* be repeated, and in the first place this happens even without the intervention of consciousness (laws of the market, crisis of overproduction).

The 'functionalist' sociologist will explain each act in terms of its contribution to the existing structure or equilibrium; and yet this same act, repeated many times, also contributes to a change from quantity to quality, i.e., to the smashing of the old system and a new 'equilibrium'. The principal characteristic of all bourgeois social science is that it does not grasp this *historical* nature of society. This is because it assumes capitalism to be a 'natural' system, corresponding to the laws of nature. Further, this contradictory nature of social reality affects consciousness, both directly through apprehension of the contradiction, and indirectly by changing the composition, organization and interrelation of the social forces (e.g., concentration of capital, proletarianization of small owners, etc); consciousness then reacts on the situation which produced it.

This is the meaning of Marx's aphorism in the third of his *Theses on Feuerbach*.

> The material doctrine concerning the changing of circumstances and upbringing forgets that circumstances are changed by men and that it is essential to educate the educator himself. This doctrine must, therefore, divide society into two parts, one of which is superior to society.
> The coincidence of the changing of circumstances and of human activity or self-changing can be conceived and rationally understood only as *revolutionary practice*.

An excellent example of the extent to which Marxists take seriously this role of consciousness is contained in Lenin's famous pamphlet *A Great Beginning* (1919):

> We all know very well the main cause of the decline in the productivity of labour that is to be observed not only in Russia, but all over the world; it is ruin and impoverishment, embitterment and weariness caused by the imperialist war, sickness and malnutrition. The latter is first in importance. Starvation — that is the cause. And in order to do away with starvation, productivity of labour must be raised in agriculture, in transport and in industry. So, we get a sort of vicious circle: in order to raise productivity of labour we must save ourselves from starvation, and in

order to save ourselves from starvation we must raise productivity of labour.

We know that in practice such contradictions are solved by breaking the vicious circle, by bringing about a radical change in the temper of the people, by the heroic initiative of the individual groups which often plays a decisive role against the background of such radical change. (Lenin *Collected Works*, Vol. 29, p, 426.)

The capacity of consciousness to actually modify the circumstances is not dependent just on strength of will and unity of purpose (although these are necessary conditions at certain definite stages), but on the level of maturity reached by all the objective forces involved. This is not an automatic relation, i.e. the revolt against certain conditions may mature before the preconditions for a new necessary order have matured, and in such cases long-term social breakdown may ensure that the 'old' development is restored once more, with certain modifications. Thus a long series of peasant wars marked the decline of feudalism.

Marxism sees itself as precisely such a necessary conscious element in history. For the already developed 'human sciences' to go further, said Marx, they must come down to analyse and to integrate with the material forces developing in the direction of the overthrow of existing conditions:

> From this moment, science, produced by the historical movement and asserting itself with it in full recognition of its cause, has ceased to be doctrinaire and has become revolutionary. (*Poverty of Philosophy*, pp. 106-107.)

Theory and practice

The origins of Marxism must be seen as the discovery of *this* relationship between theory and practice. To abstract from this process particular concepts like alienation and 'use' them or counterpose them to later concepts, as some fashionable critics do, is to destroy the essence of the development which Marx made. The *development* of Marxism after Marx's early writings has also to be grasped. It is entirely against the spirit of Marxism, though of course quite in line with the pragmatism which prevails in sociology, to go over Marx's work and its development seeking out this or that formula for current purposes. In point of fact, the adoption of a particular methodological position viz. the work of Marx, connects up, consciously or unconsciously, with the actual struggles of the class forces dealt with by Marx's theory. This is no simple process: the working class has actually gone through massive struggles, victories and defeats. The conscious grappling with these experiences and the development of Marxism is a historically unique process carried out by a definite historical organ, the revolutionary Marxist party.

To expand on this point is again to pinpoint the utter incompatibility of Marxism and sociology. Marx and his followers set out quite consciously to lead the working class. Like every revolutionary political movement, they have sought, and seek now, precisely to break the existing 'regularities' of social consciousness. Where 'sociologists' write about 'working-class culture', Marxists work towards a very different kind of 'understanding' of the working class: a conscious plan to end the situation where the conditions of capitalist exploitation form class consciousness in a dominating, chance, oppressive, spontaneous way, and to develop out of these conditions a consciously developing, challenging, theoretically and politically integrated programme of action which wins the leadership of the masses. The political party of the working class, which Marx never separates from his view of society, does not simply observe, record and 'use' information about the mentality of the mass.

Marx introduces his analysis and programme in such a way as to share the experience of the working class, to educate its most advanced and conscious section in knowledge of the structure and development of the *whole* system, not just of the life of the working class itself, to enrich theory with the sum of new experiences, to use theory as a guide to this experience, to consciously combat every influence which disrupts or attacks the unity and determination of the class or 'revises' its basic theory, etc. (democratic centralism was the organizational structure elaborated for this purpose).

The Marxist of today stands in a definite position in relation to the classes and the ideologies existing in society. He cannot present a 'sociology' of Marx, but can speak only from a revolutionary standpoint. He is writing within a situation where Marx's theories have long ago actually entered into and changed the working class and society; in the course of this Marxism itself has developed. Every Marxist of today has learned his understanding of Marx's thought through the actual struggle of political and ideological tendencies existing in the past and today.

Clearly, therefore, we cannot accept the argument of those sociologists who separate Marx's scientific insights from his philosophical outlook (e.g. C. Wright Mills). We shall, on the contrary, present the development of Marx's theory of society as a continual *deepening* of his view of 'revolutionary practice', 'the viewpoint of socialized humanity', i.e. of what the world was *becoming* through the conflict of opposites within existing capitalist society.

By its nature, then, Marxism is not a finished 'system' to be set down in even the biggest of books. It is a method by which subject and object are brought into 'identity' through struggle. The subject strives always for consciousness of the way in which it is produced by the object, of which it is part, and at the same time it brings this consciousness into conflict with the object, changing it in a more and more conscious and planned way.

'Freedom is the consciousness of necessity'. This necessity is a constantly developing process and not a predetermined plan or system. It cannot be grasped in consciousness through the preliminary mastery of some sociological scheme, supra-historical and 'general', which is then applied in each particular case. On the contrary, it can proceed only by constantly criticizing its earlier conclusions and 'predictions', negating, going beyond and at the same time building upon the earlier conceptions through grappling with the living reality. Hence Lenin's fondness for Goethe's line, 'Theory, my friend, is grey, but green is the eternal tree of life', which he used to such effect to reorientate the Bolshevik Party in April 1917.

What has often been dismissed by bourgeois historians as Lenin's 'voluntarism' or brilliant tactical sense was in fact a manifestation of the very unity of theory and practice which is at the root of Marxism. After the February Revolution of 1917 in Russia, the Bolshevik majority leadership rested complacently upon their conviction that their original programme was being confirmed in practice. They had maintained since 1905, under Lenin's guidance, that the coming bourgeois-democratic revolution could be completed only by the 'revolutionary-democratic dictatorship of the proletariat and the peasantry'. They therefore rejected Lenin's call, on his return to Petrograd in April 1917, for a strategy of overthrow of the Provisional government. Lenin replied:

> My answer is: the Bolshevik slogans and ideas *on the whole* have been confirmed by history; but *concretely* things have worked out differently;

they are more original, more peculiar, more variegated than anyone could have expected ...

This formula is already antiquated. Events have moved it from the realm of formulas into the realm of reality, clothed it with flesh and bone, concretized it and thereby modified it ...

For the present, it is essential to grasp the incontestable truth that a Marxist must take cognizance of real life, of the true facts of *reality*, and not cling to a theory of yesterday, which, like all theories, at best only outlines the main and the general, only *comes near* to embracing life in all its complexity. (*Collected Works*, Vol. 24, pp. 44-45.)

Lenin was not, of course, applying a general 'philosophical' formula directly to political tactics: he was not delivering the Bolsheviks a lecture on the materialist theory of knowledge, except insofar as it guided him in an analysis of the actual social and political situation. Here he makes a point of capital importance for the theory of social forms.

'The revolutionary-democratic dictatorship of the proletariat and peasantry' has *already* become a reality ([Lenin's footnote:] in a certain form and to a certain extent) in the Russian Revolution, for this 'formula' envisages only a *relation* of classes, and not a concrete political institution implementing this relation, this co-operation.

'The Soviet of Workers' and Soldiers' Deputies' — there you have the revolutionary-democratic dictatorship of the proletariat and the peasantry' already accomplished in reality. (*Ibid.*)

In preparing notes for this article, Lenin had written, 'the concrete Marxist proposition requires that institutions now as well as classes be taken into account'. (*Ibid*, p. 32)

Historical materialism, as Engels so often insisted, is not just the application of a general principle as the simple solution to any and every problem. It demands 'the concrete analysis of concrete conditions' (Lenin). These 'concrete conditions' are the development of definite social forms (institutions) which are necessary expressions of social consciousness, definite mechanisms of social development. Consciousness is not something standing outside of them, but develops only through them.

Trotsky, in his later writings, many times expressed the same aspects of Marxism with his warning: when your perspectives seem to be confirmed, stop and check them more carefully than ever. In other words: the very fact that a development has taken place in the objective reality requires a re-examination of that reality, an examination of the new forms produced and of the struggle of opposites within them.

After February 1917, Lenin drew attention to 'dual power' (the co-existence of the Provisional government and the Soviet of Workers' and Soldiers' Deputies) as the new and specific feature of the situation. 'Nobody previously thought of this dual power'. Here we come to the crux of his argument. The Soviets were the 'revolutionary-democratic dictatorship' envisaged in the political perspectives of the Bolsheviks. But in the situation of 1917 the petty-bourgeois peasant mass which predominated in the Soviets pushed the Soviets towards capitalism, to the other pole of the dual power, the Provisional Government of the bourgeoisie. The immediate task was therefore, for Marxists, a split in the dictatorship, a struggle for leadership of the proletariat and its allies against the prevailing majority. Those who repeated the old slogan now lagged behind the times and actually played the role of representing in the working class and within the Bolshevik Party the interests of the bourgeoisie.

'The Poverty of Philosophy'

By 1847, Marx was able to present the central ideas of his theories of society. *The Poverty of Philosophy*, his reply to Proudhon, was the first systematic statement of Marx's views on the nature of society and social classes, together with the political conclusions drawn from them, one year later stated so forcefully in the *Manifesto*. At the same time, Marx used the attack on Proudhon's speculation to make clear his settlement with Hegelian dialectics. On the basis of the method now worked out, Marx was to proceed with a lifetime of scientific work and revolutionary activity which were never at any time separated from each other. His understanding of capitalism, of the history of society, of the class struggle and politics in his own day, of the interrelations between institutions, and of the nature of ideology, were developed and refined throughout his life, in terms of his close study of the political and economic developments, particularly of the struggle of the proletariat, and of course through his untiring independent scientific endeavours.

A presentation of his ideas formulated in 1847 must of course be supplemented by the tracing out of Marx's later work, particularly in *Capital* and the preparatory work for it and in his writings on the revolutionary struggles in Europe during his lifetime. Besides his books and articles, his correspondence, especially with Engels, is invaluable.*

It would however be untrue to Marx's own approach to neglect the process which came before *The Poverty of Philosophy* and the *Manifesto*. The theories there expressed are the product of Marx's struggle to break from philosophy, more specifically from the 'left' followers of Hegel. Marx himself saw the break in a dialectical sense. In the course of rejecting Hegel's idealist dialectic, the task was to 'go beyond' it, negating it at the same time as carrying it to a higher level through the resolution of the contradiction within it (the German word *aufheben* [overcoming] expresses all these meanings at the same time).

Thus philosophy could realize itself only through ceasing to be philosophy. It could not develop further without recognizing that philosophy itself was only one aspect of social practice and could find its truth only in and through that total practice, the revolutionary activity of men in their social relations. But the division of labour which separated philosophy from its real foundations could be broken down only through revolution. Revolutionary practice was possible only by consciously bringing the conquests of philosophy into conflict with the reality of society. The key to revolution was to be found in the economic foundations of society and the class struggles produced by them.

Political economy had opened the way to this scientific view but political economy itself remained limited, just as did philosophy. Consisting of an ideological representation of capitalist society as a necessary and natural order, it ceased to represent objectively this society as soon as society was disrupted by the struggle of the working class to change it. Despite the fact that political economy had pointed to labour as the only source of wealth added to nature, it could not acknowledge the independent historical interests of the working class. Marx brought together the developments in classical political economy with the dialectic of Hegel to expose the contradictory

---

* It should in any case be said at the beginning that Engels shares with Marx the credit for laying the foundations of Marxist theory, though he himself acknowledged that Marx was the greater and more original thinker. This is not the place to answer those critics who present Engels as some positivist vulgarizer of Marx. Without question, they shared all their scientific opinions, and conducted their intellectual and political lives always in the closest collaboration, without ever discerning for themselves the differences so easily apparent to the penetrating minds of their 20th century critics.

character of capitalist society; a contradiction resolved through the unity of theory and practice in the struggle of the working class to overthrow capitalism.

He was especially concerned in *The Poverty of Philosophy* to demolish Proudhon's eclectic combination of certain abstracted conclusions of political economy, artificially selected rules of method from Hegel's dialectic, and various Utopian and reformist notions from French middle-class 'socialism'. Instead, Marx set out to show that a dynamic synthesis of the true content of political economy, Hegelian philosophy, and French socialism with its sources in the Enlightenment, realized the essence of all three and could have a future only in the revolutionary struggle of the proletariat for socialism.

Before presenting a more thorough account of the process by which this synthesis was achieved in Marx's early writings, we may summarize the essential ideas put forward in *The Poverty of Philosophy* of 1847. Not only does it define brilliantly Marx's conclusions up to that date, but it points the way forward to his own later writings in a manner which directly warns against many of the later misunderstandings of Marxist theory, not only by open enemies, but also by self-styled adherents of Marxism.

Marx expands on the third *Thesis on Feuerbach*, where, as we have seen, he had brought materialism face to face with what it had 'forgotten': 'that circumstances are changed by man'. Marx had already explained this point further in *The German Ideology* as follows:

> He (Feuerbach) does not see how the sensuous world around him is, not a thing given direct from all eternity, remaining ever the same, but the product of industry and of the state of society; and indeed, in the sense that it is an historical product, the result of the activity of a whole succession of generations, each standing on the shoulders of the preceding one, developing its industry and its intercourse, modifying its social system according to the changed needs. (*The German Ideology*. Lawrence and Wishart, London, 1965. p. 57.)

In *The Poverty of Philosophy*, Marx, answering Proudhon, now gives a brilliantly clear exposition of his concept of man as creator of his own history:

> M. Proudhon the economist understands very well that men make cloth, linen or silk materials in definite relations of production. But what he has not understood is that these definite social relations are just as much produced by men as linen, flax, etc. Social relations are closely bound up

with productive forces. In acquiring new productive forces men change their mode of production, in changing the way of earning their living, they change all their social relations. The hand-mill gives you society with the feudal lord; the steam-mill, society with the industrial capitalist.

The same men who establish their social relations in conformity with their material productivity, produce also principles, ideas and categories, in conformity with their social relations.

Thus these ideas, these categories, are as little eternal as the relations they express. They are *historical and transitory products*.

There is a continual movement of growth in productive forces, of destruction in social relations, of formation in ideas; the only immutable thing is the abstraction of movement — *mors immortalis*. (*Poverty of Philosophy*, pp. 92-93.)

Separation of thought and being had characterized mechanical materialism as well as idealism, as Hegel had pointed out ('. . . so-called realism, which takes the subjective Notion as an empty identity that absorbs the thought — determination *from without.*') Marxism, 'reading Hegel materialistically', sees concepts as developing through a practical process of transforming the reality to which they refer: thus Engels, '. . . the unity of concept and appearance manifests itself as essentially an infinite process'. (Letter to Schmidt, March 12, 1895)

This was Marx's materialism, a negation of the old 'contemplative materialism' as well as of idealism. This negation of mechanical materialism leads to the *historical materialism* which forms the underlying theme of all Marx's analytical work, especially *Capital*. All of this work is *historical* through and through. The dialectical 'laws of motion' of society are laws of motion of limited historical phenomena produced by men, enslaving them only insofar as they do not yet have the conditions to grasp this relationship, or, as in modern capitalist society, have not yet effectively built a party based on revolutionary theory to lead the working class in the objectively revolutionary situations created from time to time by capitalism.

Marx's theory itself could not have appeared except on the basis of capitalism's own historical conquests, the industrial revolution, the creation of the world market and the origin and multiplication of the proletariat, the preconditions of a system of socialized production in which men rule over economic life and not vice versa.

The theoretical conclusions of the Communists are in no way based on ideas or principles that have been invented, or discovered, by this or that would-be universal reformer. They merely express, in general terms, actual relations springing from an existing class struggle, from a historical movement going on under our very eyes. (*Communist Manifesto*)

Marx attacked Proudhon's use of dialectical concepts like 'unity of opposites', 'contradiction', etc., as mere tricks of thinking, undertaken by a petty-bourgeois intellectual who, as befitted his position between the principal classes, distributed his judgements of 'good and bad' or 'positive and negative' as so many pearls of wisdom, and then 'reunited' the opposites created by this abstraction. The principles by which the bringing together took place also derived from the bottomless barrel of petty-bourgeois moralizing. The result could only be a series of Utopian (i.e. historically abstract) constructions, for the interpretation of history as well as for the working class of the 19th century.

Marx's method was the antithesis of this. The Ancien Régime (pre-1789) in France, for example, was certainly full of contradictions, but these were 'resolved' through the struggle of the oppressed in 1789, and not by the victory of the 'good' over the 'bad' sides of the regime of the monarchy and landed nobility. Marx's comment brings out the difference between this historical materialist approach and the approach of Proudhon (which is no different from contemporary sociological theories of 'equilibrium'):

> Thus in the 18th century a number of mediocre minds were busy finding the true formula which would bring the social orders, king, nobility, parliament, etc., into equilibrium, and they woke up one morning to find that there was in fact no longer any king, nobility or parliament. The true equilibrium in this antagonism was the overthrow of all the social relations which served as a basis for these feudal existences and their antagonism.
> (Letter to Annenkov, December 28, 1846)

Capitalism's contradictions would similarly be resolved in revolution. The political conclusions for the working class were necessarily the direct antithesis of the remedies advocated by Proudhon. It was necessary, said Marx, to devote all energy to the organization and mobilization of the proletariat in its economic and political struggles into one united movement. Only through the fight for such unification of the separate struggles of the working class could their experience become part of a developing *class consciousness*, essential to their realizing their historical potential:

> Economic conditions had first transformed the mass of the people of the country into workers. The domination of capital has created for this mass a

common situation, common interests. This mass is thus already a class as against capital, but not yet for itself. In the struggle, of which we have noted only a few phases, this mass becomes united, and constitutes itself as a class for itself. The interests it defends become class interests. But the struggle of class against class is a political struggle.

In the bourgeoisie we have two phases to distinguish: that in which it constituted itself as a class under the regime of feudalism and absolute monarchy and that in which, already constituted as a class, it overthrew feudalism and monarchy to make society into a bourgeois society. The first of these phases was the longer and necessitated the greater efforts. This too began by partial combinations against the feudal lord.

Much research has been carried out to trace the different historical phases that the bourgeoisie has passed through, from the commune up to its constitution as a class. But when it is a question of making a precise study of strikes, combinations and other forms in which the proletarians carry out before our eyes their organization as a class, some are seized with real fear and others display a *transcendental* disdain. (*The Poverty of Philosophy*, pp. 145-146)

The working class will, through revolution, abolish itself and create a classless society of free producers. The state, organ of oppression by the exploiting class over the exploited, will disappear along with other forms of human alienation.

Marx's and Hegel's Dialectic

In rejecting the artificial constructions of Proudhon, Marx was proceeding from what he considered to be the 'rational kernel' of Hegel's method, which, as he expressed it, must be extracted from its idealist shell. Once this was done, said Marx, then his own method was the 'opposite' of that of Hegel. Marx means that, even while negating Hegel's 'dialectic', he at the same time 'realized' and went beyond what it had achieved. Many commentators have tried to separate out a 'scientific' or empirical contribution to sociology by Marx from his 'philosophical' ideas. However, for Marx, types of knowledge and forms of consciousness were themselves considered as social products. His materialism has at its base the concept of socially-organized labour which transforms nature, including man's own nature. How then did Marx conceive of the dialectical method?

Hegel had insisted on a Logic which was not something separate from the reality which confronted man, a Logic which was identical with the richness and movement of all reality, a Logic which expressed the whole process of man's growing consciousness of reality, and not just a dry summary of formal principles of argument, reflecting only one brief phase in the definition of reality by thinking men. Lenin notes:

> What Hegel demands is a Logic, the forms of which would be *gehaltvolle Formen* (forms with content), forms of living, real content, inseparably connected with the content. Logic is the science not of external forms of thought, but of the laws of development 'of all material, natural and spiritual things', i.e. of the development of the entire concrete content of the world and of its cognition, i.e. the sum-total, the conclusion of the 'History' of knowledge of the world. (Lenin. *Collected Works*, Vol. 38 [Philosophical Notebooks], p. 92).

Hegel believed that only the 'Absolute Idea' had reality, expressing its necessary development in nature and history. When the highest product of this natural and historical evolution, critical philosophy, grasped consciously the truth of this process, then freedom replaced necessity. For Marx, our concepts are the reflection, worked out in the history of logic and philosophy, of the objective world of nature grasped by social man in his practical struggle to survive and develop. The 'leap from necessity to freedom' is then not a matter of philosophy, not a mental act, but a practical transformation of society and nature by men who have achieved consciousness of the social necessity of revolution.

Hegel insisted that dialectics is not a master-key, a sort of set of magic numbers by which all secrets will be revealed. It is wrong to think of dialectical logic as something that is complete in itself and then 'applied' to particular examples. It is not a model of interpretation to be learned, then fitted on to reality from the outside; the task is rather to uncover the law of development of the reality itself. 'Dialectics has often been considered an *art*, as though it rested upon a subjective *talent* and did not belong to the objectivity of the Notion ...'

So long as this is the approach then we do not get beyond the limits of formal logic, considered by Hegel to be dead and fixed, rigidly insisting on the separateness of the aspects of phenomena instead of on their transitions into one another. Hegel says logic must be 'not abstract, dead and immobile, but concrete ...', and Lenin: 'This is characteristic! The spirit and essence of dialectics.' (*Ibid.*, p. 100). Consequently it is absolutely against the spirit of dialectics to artificially impose the 'triad' of thesis, antithesis, and synthesis on whatever process one chooses to abstract. Hegel is most explicit:

> That this unity, as well as the whole form of the method, is a 'triplicity' is wholly, however, the merely superficial and external side of the manner of cognition.

He goes on to say that this 'triad',

> ... has been rendered tedious and of ill-repute by the shallow misuse and the barrenness of modern so-called philosophic 'construction', which consists simply in attaching the formal framework without concept and immanent determination to all sorts of matter and employing it for external arrangement.

It is the logic of processes themselves that must be exposed. Hegel says that dialectics has often been derided as an idle play with clever concepts, whose only aim is to sceptically demonstrate the difficulties and inconsistencies of 'common sense'.

> Dialectic is generally regarded as an external and negative procedure, that does not belong to the subject matter itself, that is based on pure vanity, as a subjective craving to shake and break down what is fixed and true, or that at best leads to nothing but the inaneness of the dialectically treated matter.

When Hegel here asks for a method that 'belongs to the subject matter itself', he is not suggesting that only a description of what appears to the observer at first sight is required. Such descriptions are always couched in definite forms of thought, and are not 'pure descriptions'. It is possible to record the external characteristics of phenomena, then to arrive at judgements 'based' on these observations which in fact are an imposition on the 'facts' of some unexpressed assumption or theory. Dialectics attempts to probe to the essential self-movement of the phenomenon itself; the relations between its different aspects can then be shown as parts of a unified process, not just as separate determinations whose only interrelation is one imposed by the demands of consistency in thought. Hegel says:

> The absolute method [i.e. the method of cognition of objective truth, says Lenin] does not behave as external reflection; it draws the determinate element directly from its object itself, since it is the object's immanent principle and soul. It was this that Plato demanded of cognition, that it should 'consider things in and for themselves', and while partly considering them in their universality, it should also hold fast to them, not catching at externals, examples and comparisons, but contemplating the things alone and bringing before consciousness what is immanent in them.

This 'catching at externals, examples and comparisons' and 'generalizing' from them often parades as scientific method, particularly in the study of society and politics. Instead of the law of development of things being discovered, we get instead a neat or 'consistent' arrangement of abstracted characteristics of similar phenomena. Hegel's criticism of this method is extremely sharp:

> That procedure of knowledge reflecting on experience, which first 'perceives' determinations in the phenomenon, next makes them the basis, and assumes for their so-called 'explanation' corresponding 'fundamental materials' or 'forces' which are supposed to produce these determinations of the phenomenon . . .

What is advanced as an explanation of a thing turns out to be only 'determination deduced from that for which they are meant to be the grounds — hypotheses and figments derived by an uncritical reflection.'

Against this flat and 'uncritical' method, in essence tautological, Hegel asserts his own:

> Thinking Reason (as compared with 'imagination' and 'intelligent reflection'), sharpens the blunt differences of Variety, the mere manifold of imagination, into essential difference, that is, Opposition. The manifold entities acquire activity and vitality in relation to one another only when driven on to the sharp point of Contradiction; thence they draw negativity, which is the inherent pulsation of self-movement and vitality . . .

Hegel's dialectical method is often condemned as an accommodation to the 'status quo', because of its insistence on the 'identity of thought and the object'. But it is only *idealism* which condemns the dialectic to becoming a dead *system* in this way. The following quotations explain further the 'dynamic' and 'critical' nature of dialectical knowledge, once Hegel is 'read materialistically' (Lenin):

> The self-identity of the Idea is one with the 'process'; and the thought which frees actuality from the semblance of purposeless changeability and transfigures it into the Idea must not imagine this truth of actuality as a dead repose or bare 'picture', matt, without impulse or motion, or as a genius, number, or abstract thought. In the Idea the Notion reaches freedom, and because of this the Idea contains also the 'harshest opposition'; its repose consists in the security and certainty with which it eternally creates and eternally overcomes it, coinciding in it with itself.

Lenin shows what Marx took from this method, rewriting the passage as follows:

The coincidence of thought with the object is a *process*: thought (=man) must not imagine truth in the form of dead repose, in the form of a bare picture (image), pale (matt), without impulse, without motion, like a genius, like a number, like abstract thought. The idea contains also the strongest contradiction, repose (for man's thought) consists in the firmness and certainty with which he eternally creates (this contradiction between thought and object) and eternally overcomes it ...

Finally, Lenin rewrites the passage:

Cognition is the eternal, endless approximation of thought to the object. The 'reflection' of nature in man's thought must be understood not 'lifelessly', not 'abstractly', not 'devoid of movement, not without contradictions', but in the eternal 'process' of movement, the arising of contradictions, and their solution. (*Ibid.* pp. 194-5)

Despite Hegel's insistence that the dialectic must take into account the constant state of change of all reality, his own philosophy became an adaptation to the existing political set-up in Germany. This came about not because of the dialectical character of his thought, but because he remained an idealist, considering the activity of the mind, the movement of ideas, to be the essential reality, with the material world only its external passing form. As Marx said:

In its mystified form, dialectic became the fashion in Germany, because it seemed to transfigure and to glorify the existing state of things. In its rational form it is a scandal and abomination to bourgeoisdom and its doctrinaire professors, because it includes in its comprehension an affirmative recognition of the existing state of things, at the same time, also, the recognition of the negation of that state, of its inevitable breaking up; because it regards every historically developed social form as in fluid movement and therefore takes into account its transient nature not less than its momentary existence; because it lets nothing impose upon it, and it is in essence critical and revolutionary. (Karl Marx, Preface to the Second Edition of *Capital*, Vol. I)

For Hegel the subject-matter of philosophy was thought itself and the history of thought. He did not realise that for philosophers to concentrate only on this aspect of man's conscious existence was itself a form of 'alienation', an expression of the class society which divides men into 'thinkers' and 'workers', obscuring the essential unity and interdependence of their various activities, distorting each individual to the needs of a class-dominated mode of production. For all his brilliance in analysing the forms of thought, and in criticizing the rigidity of formal logic, Hegel remained imprisoned by philosophy itself. His life's work, a great feat of critical scholarship, exposed the limits, interrelations and contradictions of previous philosophies and systems of logic, but the solution he offered was a false one: so long as he remained an idealist, Marx insisted, his 'solution' was purely in the realm of ideas, of philosophy itself. The philosopher could be satisfied with his rational and dynamic picture of the evolution of notions — but the real social world which created these notions and their movement remained as solidly in existence as before. Because the activity of man is taken by Hegel to be purely mental activity, then the philosophical act of transcending existing concepts is a complete victory for reason and freedom; the conquest of alienation and false consciousness can be achieved purely in the realm of thought.

In his *Economic and Philosophical Manuscripts of 1844* (Lawrence and Wishart, London 1959) the youthful Marx strove to expose this fundamental weakness of the idealist dialectic: in his philosophy, said Marx, Hegel goes beyond ('supersedes' or 'transcends') the existing ideas of men; but he considers these ideas purely as thought-forms and not as part of human practice:

> ... Hegel 'supersedes' in philosophy ... therefore not 'real' religion, the 'real' state, or 'real' nature but religion itself already become an object of knowledge, i.e., Dogmatics; the same with Jurisprudence, Political Science and Natural Science. (p. 163)

In other words the Hegelian might develop a thoroughgoing critique of existing theories of say, the State, developing out of their contradictions a more consistent theory. But if the process stops there, the real state remains unaltered, not superseded. Indeed, to 'confine' theory to the successful criticism of other theories of the State amounts objectively to preventing the conscious action that is required to change the actual State.

In Hegel therefore all the laws of the dialectic remain locked within pure speculative philosophy. Marx, on the other hand, saw the history of man and his consciousness as the developing active force of labour, of the practice of social man in his necessary conquest of nature. In 'production', man expressed his nature as part of the objective world. Instead of speculating about what 'human nature' or 'the essence of man' might be, we should recognize that the history of human 'industry' is 'an open book of the human faculties', a ready-made basis for a scientific psychology, as he wrote a little later. Instead of seeing history as the 'realization' of some abstract 'self-consciousness' of man, it was necessary to study it as the creation and emergence of man's self-consciousness through his developing material practice. This was how Marx first criticized Hegel materialistically:

> Hegel makes man the man of self-consciousness instead of making self-consciousness the self-consciousness of man, of the real man, and therefore a man living also in a real objective world and determined by that world. ('Critique of the Hegelian Dialectic' in *Economic and Philosophical Manuscripts of 1844*)

Philosophy, appearing and flourishing in that phase of social evolution which brought the divorce of mental from manual labour, ignored the practical root of all thought and tried to examine thought as such. From this point of view, with pure thought seen as the essence of man, the objective world could only be 'understood' as an alienated form of self-consciousness. According to the Hegelians, once this alienated form has been grasped as Idea, then it has been mastered, the alienation has been overcome. The objective world is nothing but a 'negative' form of self-consciousness itself. Once this is grasped dialectically, the alienated form, the negation, returns to the essential self-consciousness of man. The negation is itself negated. A scientific view of society, on the other hand, must see the active forces of real men in society as the means of changing reality. To change one's 'ideas' about the reality can only be part of this process. As Marx summarized it: 'The weapon of criticism is replaced by the criticism of weapons'; by this he meant that existing institutions would be changed by social 'forces' within the society producing them and not by the blows of philosophy, however 'critical'. The theory of society founded by Marx has no room for philosophy of the old 'speculative' type, based on the idea of independently moving thought, with a subject-matter and development of its own, independent of reality but sometimes descending to impinge upon it. By Marx's day, the achievements of political economy, science and logic had laid the necessary basis upon which the development of humanity itself could be viewed as objectively as any natural process instead of being the subject of speculation. As Marx put it in *The German Ideology:*

> Where speculation ends — in real life — there real, positive science begins: the representation of the practical activity, of the practical process of development of men. Empty talk about consciousness ceases, and real knowledge has to take its place. When reality is depicted, philosophy as an independent branch of activity loses its medium of existence. (*The German Ideology.* p. 38.)

From then on it was a question of grasping in consciousness the motive forces of the development of the material life of man.

> Men can be distinguished from animals by consciousness, by religion or anything else you like. They themselves begin to distinguish themselves from animals as soon as they begin to 'produce' their means of subsistence, a step which is conditioned by their physical organisation. By producing their means of subsistence men are indirectly producing their actual material life. (*Ibid.*, p. 31.)

The existence of the working class, in struggle against capitalism, is the basis of the possibility of ending that state of affairs where man's product dominates him through the power of the ruling class. 'Alienation' will be conquered by the overthrow of capitalism; in a socialist economy men will put to their own planned use all the products of human history. Contrast this with Hegel: his 'philosophical' conquest of alienation amounted to 're-appropriating' to men the objective world by destroying its objectivity, by seeing it as purely an expression of self-consciousness, by grasping it only in thought. Its objectivity had to be destroyed, because it was precisely in this respect that it failed to coincide with the 'essence' of man, subjectivity, self-consciousness. For Marx, this 'essence' is only the historical practical activity of men in definite production relations.

A materialist dialectic, of the kind which Marx always wanted to find the time to write, and for which Lenin deliberately laid the groundwork in his Notebooks on Hegel, must therefore reverse the picture given by Hegel of the relation between the forms of thought and the history of nature and society. The evolution of thought, the origin and development of logic and science, must be seen in their total context as the outgrowth and a vital part of the development of man's practice, his organization in society to develop and explore the techniques at his disposal for the conquest of nature. Not only the science of history, above all that economic history which was to all intents and purposes a closed book before Marx, but also a scientific psychology will be necessary for the development and deepening of materialist dialectics:

The history of philosophy, *ERGO:* | briefly, the history of cognition in general
| the whole field of knowledge

Greek Philosophy indicated all these moments	The history of the separate sciences	} these are the fields of knowledge from which the theory of knowledge and dialectics should be built
	"　　"　　" the mental development of the child	
	"　　"　　" the mental development of animals	
	" *language* NB: + psychology + physiology of the sense organs	

(Lenin, Philosophical Notebooks, *Collected Works*, Vol. 38, pp. 352-3)

The dialectical materialist theory of knowledge, the science of human thought, is thus the scientific history of the material foundations, origins and development of the actual 'thinking' of men, which goes on in the context of man's practice, first of all in production.

What man contemplates in philosophy (his own thought), according to Marx, is the reflection of an objective world partly produced by his own 'labour'. Man 'duplicates himself not only, as in consciousness, intellectually, but also actively, in reality, and therefore he contemplates himself in a world that he has created.' (*Economic and Philosophical Manuscripts of 1844*, p. 76.)

It has been pointed out that it was in the most abstract sphere of logic and philosophy that the dialectic was first elaborated, and only later worked out for human society and for nature. What happened, then, was that abstract thought — an abstraction from experience at one level — enriched itself by taking on more and more of the concrete, objective world with which thought grappled. It was Marx who turned dialectics in this direction through his concept of human activity not just as 'critical thought' but as 'revolutionary practice'. Hegel had already indicated that to obtain real objectivity, cognition must reach the point at which it actually realizes itself in 'the Practical Idea': consciousness develops into freedom through incorporating into itself the 'necessities' of the external world; subject and object are united. In his *Theses on Feuerbach* (1845) Marx gave his version of this problem of the objectivity of thought:

> The question whether objective (*gegenständliche*) truth can be attributed to human thinking is not a question of theory but is a 'practical' question. In practice man must prove the truth, that is, the reality and power, the

this-sidedness (*Diesseitigkeit*) of his thinking. The dispute over the reality or non-reality of thinking which is isolated from practice is a purely 'scholastic' question.

For the development of an abstract consciousness, Marx substituted the creative activity (*praxis*) of man in his social relations of production. The elaboration of the Marxist theory of history and society would consist of the presentation of human experience in this framework.

Hegel had shown that all thinking goes through similar phases, proceeding from an abstract, partial appreciation to a richer and more nearly complete reflection of the real phenomena in all their transitions, transformations and interrelations. Further examination of the transition from 'philosophy' to Marxism may bring out more clearly the character of Marx's dialectical method.

In describing the 'laws' of the movement of thought from appearance to essence and to 'the notion', Hegel tries to take into his logical system all earlier elaborations of the problem. He aims to transcend (i.e., to negate, to go beyond, but at the same time incorporate) these earlier philosophies by showing them to be only one-sided, exaggerated, abstracted parts or aspects of an infinitely rich, developing whole of which the parts are only phases, which can be truly grasped only in their developing and contradictory relations to one another and to the whole.

What is this 'thought', whose evolution and anatomy Hegel so brilliantly describes, tracing the course of its work in all the sectors of human scholarship and creation? It is the thought of living, active men, existing in concrete social relations; it is part of their practice in these surroundings; it reflects their growing control over nature and the contradictions in the social relations within which this control is organized. In the course of conquering nature men are forced to strive for a more thorough, a deeper and more concrete understanding of it. Their ideas of nature begin as the crudest and most 'subjective' abstractions, based first on fleeting impressions and on the immediate and pressing needs of subsistence. Those aspects of the environment which are organized in this early type of thought are 'selected' from the environment, 'significance' allotted to them, and the relations between them conceived, not scientifically but subjectively. This is borne out by investigations of the ideas of primitive societies and of early child development. As the organization of men in society advances in its handling of the problems of production, knowledge grows and is refined in order to conform with the actual structure and development of the external world, through a process of checking in hundreds of generations of experience. Concepts are broadened, or broken down into more limited and strictly defined concepts in order to take into account new or newly encountered phenomena, distinctions are made which more accurately reflect the essential relations in nature. The history of science is a central component of dialectics as a theory of knowledge. (We are giving a general summary. There is not of course a gradual, non-contradictory evolution of positive knowledge.)

But all knowledge is organized in concepts or ideas; it is worked through the mental activities of men. Dialectical materialism of course recognizes this, but rejects the idealist conclusion that the essential reality is thought itself. Engels showed long ago that this conceptual character of all knowledge must not in any way lead to a separation of thought and the objective world which it reflects. The ability to work with concepts is itself something which has developed in material relations with the world, and must itself be understood dialectically.

> In any case natural science has now advanced so far that it can no longer escape the dialectical synthesis. But it will make this process easier for itself if it does not lose sight of the fact that the results in which its experiences are summarized are concepts; but that the art of working with concepts is not inborn and also is not given with ordinary everyday consciousness, but requires real thought, and that this thought similarly has a long empirical history, not more and not less than empirical natural science. Only by learning to assimilate the results of the development of philosophy during the past two and a half thousand years will it be able to rid itself on the one hand of any isolated natural philosophy standing apart from it, outside it, and above it, and on the other hand also of its own limited method of thought, which was its inheritance from English empiricism. (F. Engels, *Anti-Dühring*, Preface to 2nd Edition, p. 19.)

This passage brings out very clearly the implications of a dialectical approach to method not only in natural science but also in politics. Marx and his followers consider that they are obliged to fight always to understand the history of their own ideas and the movement of which those ideas are part and that without a critical development of these ideas in struggle, would-be Marxists will remain victims, theoretically and politically, of the concepts and methods of bourgeois thought with all its political consequences.

Men's thoughts, then, can never grasp the whole of concrete reality. Their concepts develop by learning ways of reflecting the real movement of the world. Only the infinite (i.e., never completed) sum of all abstractions would give the concrete in all its completeness. The dialectical method is a development from formal and everyday logical thinking in such a way as to comprehend the changing and contradictory, infinitely-sided character of natural and social processes:

> Dialectical thinking is related to vulgar thinking in the same way that a motion picture is related to a still photograph. The motion picture does not outlaw the still photograph but combines a series of them according to the laws of motion. Dialectics does not deny the syllogism (of formal logic), but teaches us to combine syllogisms in such a way as to bring our understanding closer to the eternally changing reality. Hegel in his *Logic* established a series of laws: change of quantity into quality, development through contradictions, conflict of content and form, interruption of continuity, change of possibility into inevitability, etc., which are just as important for theoretical thought as is the simple syllogism for more elementary tasks. (L.D. Trotsky, *In Defence of Marxism*, New Park Publications, 1966, pp. 50-51.)

The history of philosophy is one aspect of the development of human social practice. But philosophy's specific task is to sum up the most general laws of thought. Hegel's dialectical picture of thought claimed to be more than this. It claimed to be a picture of the essential reality, the reality of the Absolute Idea of which the material world of nature is but the outward show. Surveying and analysing the history of thought, Hegel took the laws of its development, taking into itself (as knowledge) more and more of the concrete as it developed, to be the laws of development of Reality. This illusion of completeness and correctness of the idealist dialectical theory of knowledge is strengthened precisely because correct thought does develop by reflecting the material world! The more man investigates and controls nature, the richer and more subtle becomes his knowledge, the more flexible and all-sided become his concepts. Hegel thought that all this was the discovery of the flowering of the Absolute Idea, independently generating all of these things. The role of human thought was to 'understand' the necessity and the lawfulness of this product of the Absolute Idea in the vulgar material world, which should be understood as the Appearance through which thought must penetrate to the ideal reality behind it. Once all the material of thought was conquered in this way, grasped as a manifestation of the Absolute Idea, 'criticism' would have done its work and given to man his 'freedom', the consciousness of necessity.

But the 'proof' of the correctness of Hegel's idealist dialectic only became possible through the results of hundreds of millions of practical actions carried out by human beings in their social relations acting on nature and, in the course of this, changing their social relations and thereby themselves. The reason for the development of human knowledge, including philosophy, to science and dialectics, is that man's practice on the objective world brings his concepts closer to the real behaviour of that world. There is thus a 'materialist' explanation of the completeness and correctness of Hegel's dialectical logic, as well as of its limitations. Once this dialectical logic is consciously developed, as with Hegel, it is forced to the consideration of the vital role of 'practice'. The development of philosophy itself, since its stock-in-trade is 'ideas' and 'explanations', inevitably goes forward to dialectical materialism, to the recognition of itself as only one 'moment' in the conquest of the objective world by socially organized man. Then philosophy can be seen as the highest form of the role played by abstract thought during the period of the separation of mental from manual labour, the period of class society. In order to advance, philosophy must become the theoretical weapon of the class which goes beyond the limits of this period, just as the proletariat requires the most advanced logic in order to grasp its own role. Henceforth the scientifically-based struggle to transform nature and society, and the investigation of the conditions and theories of this transformation, constitute the material of the central intellectual activity of man. In all these spheres 'revolutionizing practice' is the central concept. In this sense, Marx, when 'standing Hegel on his feet', represents the qualitative stage in the development of philosophy prepared by all the quantitative advances of the Classical German school within the idealist framework, filled out above all by Hegel. But this theoretical advance was only part, and had to be consciously grasped as 'part', of a qualitative stage in the development of society, of the class struggle: of the revolutionization of society by the proletariat in preparation for that stage of history when the role of human activity is consciously grasped and rationally planned, freed from social illusions, based on an understanding of the necessary relations between men and their environment.

II
The materialist conception of history: part one

Marx's materialism

Marx's theory of history cannot be separated in any way from his political programme of the proletarian revolution. For this reason, it has always been subjected to attack from 'orthodox' theories of history and sociology, as well as from the political opponents of Communism.

The attacks on Marxism fall into two main categories: those which understand Marxism as 'economic determinism' (and this includes some self-styled advocates of Marxism), and those which see Marxism only as an 'ideology' of the working class. From both sides we have a misreading of the nature of Marx's *materialism*. Marx differentiated himself, as we have seen, from the old 'contemplative materialism', with its standpoint of the isolated individual in 'civil society'. A series of commentators on Marx from Lukács onwards have taken this as a rejection of materialism.

Marx asserted many times and without equivocation that his outlook was *materialist* in character, and that without grasping this, his conception of history could not be understood. Whatever later critics may think of the 'metaphysical' character of all materialism, Marx himself was explicit, and his position does not change on this fundamental question from *The German Ideology* (1846) to long after the publication of *Capital*. In his Preface to the Second Edition of *Capital* (1873), Marx refers to the preface to his earlier *Critique of Political Economy* (1859) as a discussion of 'the materialistic basis of my method (*die materialistische Grundlage meiner Methode*),' and he states later:

> My dialectic method is not only different from the Hegelian, but is its direct opposite. To Hegel, the life-process of the human brain, i.e., the process of thinking, which, under the name of 'the Idea', he even trans-

forms into an independent subject, is the demiurgos of the real world, and the real world is only the external form of 'the Idea'. With me, on the contrary, the ideal is nothing else than the material world reflected by the human mind, and transformed into forms of thought. (*Capital*, Volume I, p. 19)

It should be noted that this 1873 Preface consists of a reply to a favourable review: Marx objects *only* to the reviewer's opinion that whereas his (Marx's) method is 'realistic', his presentation is 'idealistic' in the Hegelian manner.

Marx's whole purpose here is to make clear that he is a thoroughgoing materialist: hence the explicit statement about 'the material world reflected by the human mind, and translated into forms of thought.' We may go back beyond even *The German Ideology* to the *Economic and Philosophical Manuscripts* (1844), for several statements on materialism quite consistent with this, among them the following:

> History itself is a real part of natural history — of nature's coming to be man. Natural science will in time subsume under itself the science of man, just as the science of man will subsume under itself natural science: there will be one science. (*Economic and Philosophical Manuscripts* (1844), p. 11.)

Similarly, Marx retained, while writing *Capital*, the opinion he held in the 1844 period, that Hegel's dialectical laws were correct reflections of the behaviour of nature, *including* human society. In Vol. I of *Capital* he writes:

> The possessor of money or commodities actually turns into a capitalist only where the maximum sum advanced for production greatly exceeds the maximum of the middle ages. Here, as in natural science, is shown the correctness of the law discovered by Hegel (in his *Logic*), that merely quantitative differences beyond a certain point pass into qualitative changes. (p. 296)

(Those who like to portray Engels as an illegitimate 'innovator' in the use of Marx's dialectic to explain natural science are careful to avoid this and similar passages.)

Only six years before his death, Marx wrote against those, '. . . who want to give socialism a "higher, idealistic" orientation, that is to say, to replace its materialistic basis (which demands serious objective study from anyone who tries to use it) . . .' (Letter to Sorge, October 19, 1877)

Marx was not in the habit of using words like 'materialist' loosely, and in all these passages he is specifically rejecting tendencies towards, or allegations of idealism.

What Marx criticized in the earlier materialism (which had its highest expression in the German philosopher of the 1830s and 1840s, Feuerbach) was its separation from history, the history of real, living men in their social relations, acting upon the world. He continued to criticize the natural scientists for this same gap, for the abstractness of their materialism; thus in 1867:

> It is, in reality, much easier to discover by analysis the earthly core of the misty creations of religion, than, conversely, it is to develop from the actual relations of life the corresponding celestialized forms of those relations. The latter method is the only *materialistic*, and therefore the only scientific one. The weak points in the *abstract materialism* of natural science, a materialism that excludes history and its process, are at once evident from the abstract and ideological conceptions of its spokesmen, whenever they venture beyond the bounds of their own speciality. (*Capital*, Vol.I, p. 367) (My emphasis, C.S.)

So long as materialism remained abstracted from history in this way, Marx considered that it was incomplete and inconsistent. The understanding of this material relation between man and the rest of nature, a relation effected by production in definite social relations, was the necessary extension of philosophical materialism; but at this very point it ceases to be *philosophical* materialism, because philosophy is recognized as one of the alienated products of man's productive activity, at the same time continuing to understand and transforming their activity. The passage which explains these points most adequately is to be found in *The German Ideology* (1846), at the point where Marx and Engels elaborate on their *Theses on Feuerbach*. The opening sentence below is an early verdict on the later attempts to distinguish their 'naturalism' (i.e. their outlook in the 1840s) from materialism:

> Of course, in all this the priority of external nature remains unassailed, and all this has no application to the original men produced by *generatio aequivoca* (spontaneous generation): but this differentiation has meaning only in so far as man is considered to be distinct from nature. For that matter, nature, the nature that preceded human history, is not by any means the nature in which Feuerbach lives, not the nature which today no longer exists anywhere (except perhaps on a few Australian coral-islands of recent origin) and which, therefore, does not exist for Feuerbach.
> Certainly Feuerbach has a great advantage over the 'pure' materialists in that he realizes how man too is an 'object of the senses'. But apart from the fact that he only conceives him as an 'object of the senses', not as 'sensuous activity', because he still remains in the realm of theory and conceives of

men not in their given social connection, not under their existing conditions of life, which have made them what they are, he never arrives at the really existing active men, but stops at the abstraction 'man', and gets no further than recognizing 'the true, individual, corporeal man' emotionally, i.e., he knows no other 'human relationships' 'of man to man' than love and friendship, and even then idealized. He gives no criticism of the present conditions of life. Thus he never manages to conceive the sensuous world as the total living sensuous activity of the individuals composing it; and therefore when, for example, he sees instead of healthy men a crowd of scrofulous, over-worked and consumptive starvelings, he is compelled to take refuge in the 'higher perception' and in the ideal 'compensation in the species', and thus to relapse into idealism at the very point where the communist materialist sees the necessity, and at the same time the condition, of a transformation both of industry and of the social structure.
As far as Feuerbach is a materialist he does not deal with history, and as far as he considers history he is not a materialist. With him materialism and history diverge completely, a fact which incidentally is already obvious from what has been said. (*The German Ideology*, pp. 58-59)

The nature of social relations

One of the criticisms directed against Marx is that he never wrote a systematic account of his theory of history, with a general exposition of central concepts like 'class' or 'relations of production'. This task was later undertaken by Labriola, Plekhanov and others. But the criticism is misplaced, in the sense that everything Marx and Engels wrote was an elaboration of historical materialism, and this applies particularly to *Capital* itself, described by Lenin as a scientific test of the materialist conception of history.

Marx came closest to a general summary of his theory of history in the famous Preface to the *Critique of Political Economy* (1859). The brevity and confidence of the formulations in this Preface are deceptive. They are the conclusion of the development from philosophy which we have briefly outlined and which greatly illuminates their meaning. In their struggle against idealism and mechanical materialism in philosophy, Marx and Engels had very early begun a study of the development of political economy and the history of the class struggle. This, of course, followed necessarily from their philosophical conclusions: to replace speculation and metaphysics with the scientific study of objective developments.

The materialist conception of history represented a synthesis of the highest developments in German idealist philosophy, British political economy, and social and political theory and history in France. Working as they did in the atmosphere of 'left' Hegelianism, an extreme expression of the particularly 'philosophical' and speculative way in which the weak German bourgeoisie developed, Marx and Engels were compelled to do battle against highly abstract notions of man and his activity.

But they could not proceed on the basis of materialism as they found it. Marx's advance beyond the old philosophical materialism enabled him to present social relations as a *product* of human social activity, and not only as an 'environment' influencing or restricting the activity of individuals. It was only when Marx had arrived at this understanding of social activity, production, as the basis of the relation between consciousness and existence, that he could himself completely shed the 'humanism' of Feuerbach, who continued to see man as some 'abstract being, squatting outside the world'; this 'abstract' materialism forced Feuerbach to view the 'essence' of man as something timeless and unhistorical.

> Feuerbach resolves the religious essence into the 'human' essence. But the human essence is no abstraction inherent in each single individual. In its reality it is the ensemble of the social relations.
>
> Feuerbach, who does not enter upon a criticism of this real essence, is consequently compelled:
>
> 1. To abstract from the historical process and to fix the religious sentiment (*Gemüt*) as something by itself and to presuppose an abstract — 'isolated' — human individual.
>
> 2. The human essence, therefore, can with him be comprehended only as 'genus', as an internal, dumb generality which merely *naturally* unites the many individuals. (*Theses on Feuerbach*, No. VI)

For Marx, then, 'the human essence' is 'the ensemble [totality] of the social relations'. It is this totality and not the 'natural' similarity of men which unites the individuals. It is the material process of production and interaction which constantly recreates this unity. Hegel saw all this as the 'expression' or alienation of self-consciousness. Marx saw self-consciousness as one of the 'alienated' products of this material process. It was thus that he 'stood Hegel on his feet'. Meanwhile the 'left Hegelians' were trying to preserve the independence of speculative philosophy and theology against this discovery. Marx was very harsh with them:

> Once man is apprehended as the essence, the basis of all human activity

and situations, only 'criticism' can invent new categories and transform man himself into a category and into the principle of a whole new series of categories as it is doing now. It is true that in so doing it steps on to the only road to salvation that remained for terrorized and persecuted *theological* humanity. History does nothing, it 'possesses no immense wealth', it 'wages no battles'. It is *man*, real living man, that does all that, that possesses and fights; 'history' is not a person apart, using man as a means for its own particular aims; history is nothing but the activity of man pursuing his aims. (*The Holy Family*, Lawrence & Wishart 1956, p. 125)

For this abstraction of 'History' Feuerbach had substituted 'man', but so long as even this 'man' was still conceived unhistorically, materialism could not yet be consistent.

The criticism of Feuerbach was completed in *The German Ideology*, where Marx and Engels made a long, unfinished draft outline of their historical theory:

This conception of history depends on our ability to expound the real process of production, starting out from the material production of life itself, and to comprehend the form of intercourse connected with this and created by this mode of production (i.e., civil society in its various stages), as the basis of all its history; and to show it in its action as state, to explain all the different theoretical products and forms of consciousness, religion, philosophy, ethics, etc. etc, and trace their origins and growth from that basis; by which means, of course, the whole thing can be depicted in its totality (and therefore, too, the reciprocal action of these various sides on one another). (pp. 49-50)

It should be noted here that Marx and Engels insisted on the 'reciprocal actions of these various sides on one another' as part of the totality just as explicitly as Engels did in his letters of the 1890s, which have sometimes been misinterpreted or misrepresented as an 'admission' that the materialist theory had been wrong or one-sided. This conception of history is put forward as the answer to all the speculation about the 'essence' of man:

This sum of productive forces, capital funds and social forms of intercourse, which every individual and generation finds in existence as something given, is the real basis of what the philosophers have conceived as 'substance' and 'essence of man', and what they have defied and attacked ... (*Ibid.*, p. 50)

Once this approach to history was worked out, Marx and Engels insisted on its being *used*, and not simply reasserted, and this more than anything else explains the absence of a 'textbook' by Marx or Engels on historical materialism.

Although Marx was to devote almost the whole of his life to the economic analysis in *Capital*, he had the original intention of analysing and presenting the history of all the principal social and ideological forms developed by capitalism, as well as the outlines of pre-capitalist forms of production. The analysis of capitalism, as of any other socio-economic formation, must consist of specific historical investigation; the lesson driven home against Feuerbach, that men were united by specific social-production relations, an objective reality open to a scientific study, must be held fast as the key to history.

In *The Poverty of Philosophy* Marx re-emphasizes this point in a way which contrasts with the approach of bourgeois sociology, with its starting points of interaction between individuals, 'unit-acts', etc. Proudhon wrote about 'Society' as something independent of the men comprising it, and gave this abstraction the name 'Prometheus.' Marx breaks down the abstraction and concludes:

> What then, ultimately, is this Prometheus resuscitated by M. Proudhon? It is society, social relations based on class antagonism. These relations are not relations between individual and individual, but between worker and capitalist, between farmer and landlord, etc. Wipe out these relations and you annihilate all society, and your Prometheus is nothing but a ghost without arms or legs . . .(p. 84)

If we add to this the passage quoted earlier to the effect that productive forces, production relations and the ideas produced in conformity with them, are themselves 'historical and transitory products', we find a view of society in complete contrast to the sociological theories of 'social structure' as some sort of 'bony framework' to which institutions adhere or to whose stability they functionally contribute.

Marx's insistence on the need to start from the historically *specific* character of social relations in each historically-developed mode of production is also first made clear in the polemic against Proudhon. Where Proudhon thought he was dealing with property as such, he should have been analysing *bourgeois* property, its historical origin, development and limits. Marx shows that it was not a question of 'criticizing property', but of seeing that history itself had 'criticized' property, by eliminating first slave, then feudal property, and replacing them with capitalist private property.

> The question of what this (bourgeois private property) is could only have been answered by a critical analysis of '*political* economy', embracing these

property relations as a whole, not in their legal expression as voluntary relations, but in their real form, that is, as relations of production. But as he entangled the whole of these economic relations to the general juristic conception of 'property', Proudhon could not get beyond the answer which Brissot, in a similar work, had already, before 1789, given in the same words: 'Property is theft'. (Letter to Schweitzer, January 24, 1865)

This historical view distinguishes Marxism from orthodox sociology. But this is not an abstract historicism. Each social order is characterized by specific social antagonisms, rooted in the economy, and it is through these antagonisms, each of which must be concretely studied and analysed, that men make their own history. In his mature work, Marx was just as insistent on this as he had been earlier. The following passages from the uncompleted volumes of *Capital* are the clearest statement of this position. Men themselves are the active force who, through their social relationships and contradictions, transform society and bring about transitions from one historical epoch to another. This conception is in complete contrast to all bourgeois sociology.

The specific economic form, in which unpaid surplus labour is pumped out of direct producers, determines the relationship of rulers and ruled, as it grows directly out of production itself, and, in turn, reacts upon it as a determining element. Upon this, however, is founded the entire formation of the economic community which grows up out of the production relations themselves, thereby simultaneously its specific political form. It is always the direct relationship of the owners of the conditions of production to the direct producers — a relation always naturally corresponding to a definite stage in the development of the methods of labour and thereby its social productivity — which reveals the innermost secret, the hidden basis of the entire social structure, and with it the political form of the relation of sovereignty and dependence, in short, the corresponding form of the state. This does not prevent the same economic basis — the same from the standpoint of its main conditions — due to innumerable different empirical circumstances, natural environment, racial relations, external historical influences, etc., from showing infinite variations and gradations in appearance, which can only be ascertained by analysis of the empirically given circumstances. (*Capital*, Volume III, Lawrence and Wishart, 1960, p. 772)

What is important here is not the concluding warning of the need to analyse the 'infinite' variations on the same economic base, so much as the conception of a totality of relations based upon exploitation, upon an antagonistic clash of material interests. In Vol. II of the same work,

Marx explains that in the better-known first volume his economic analysis has taken as its basis the objective conflict of classes and its movement. The dialectic is not a system of concepts like 'totality' and 'negation' imposed on the material, but a method of exposing the contradictory developments of the material itself:

> Whatever the social form of production, labourers and means of production always remain factors of it. But in a state of separation from each other either of these factors can be such only potentially. For production to go on at all they must unite. The specific manner in which this union is accomplished distinguishes the different economic epochs of the structure of society from one another. In the present case, the separation of the free worker from his means of production is the starting-point given, and we have seen how and under what conditions these two elements are united in the hands of the capitalist, namely, as the productive mode of existence of his capital. (pp. 34-35)

In the years immediately following 1847, Marx and Engels had ample opportunity to demonstrate their theories, first in the elaboration of their political programme (*The Communist Manifesto*), and then in the analysis of the historical forces at work in the European revolutions of 1848, from which they drew the detailed lessons for the working-class movement. Lenin said of Marx's writings on the nature of the state in 1848-1851: 'Here as everywhere, his teaching is the summary of experience, illuminated by a profound philosophical conception of the world and a rich knowledge of history.' (*The State and Revolution*).

Marx and Engels were convinced that, besides following all developments in scholarship and research, they must above all enrich their theory of history through the experience of the class struggle, which their opponents, as Marx had said, treated with 'transcendental disdain'. Marx paid great attention to the strategic and tactical lessons of the 1848-1851 events as an integral part of the application to them of his theory of historical materialism. We shall return to these matters when dealing with the specific questions of class, political power and revolution. In this chapter, Marx's writings on the 1848 Revolution enter only to illuminate the general theory described in the 1859 'Preface' to the *Contribution to the Critique of Political Economy*.

(Just as Marx in 1848, and later in 1871, developed his theory in line with what was for him the central question, the class struggle, so today a Marxist presentation of historical materialism would require documentation and development from the rich and complex history of this struggle in this century, together with a critical account of the theoretical appraisal of it in the Marxist movement. Such a presentation is not possible in the space of this volume. The works of Lenin and Trotsky are the basis of this development of historical materialism.)

The 1859 'Preface'

Marx begins his 1859 summary: 'In the social production of their life, men enter into definite relations that are indispensable and independent of their will, relations of production which correspond to a definite stage of development of their productive forces. The sum total of these relations of production constitutes the economic structure of society, the real foundation, on which rises a legal and political superstructure and to which correspond definite forms of social consciousness. The mode of production of material life conditions the social, political and intellectual life process in general. It is not the consciousness of men that determines their being, but, on the contrary, their social being that determines their consciousness.'

We should especially note Marx saying that it is *'The sum total* ["*totality*"] *of these relations of production'* which 'constitutes *the economic structure* of society, *the real foundation* etc.' A long controversy in the USSR in the late 1940s was 'settled', with appropriate pronouncements by Stalin, to the effect that the implements or techniques of production were the most basic, the most 'mobile', element in the mode of production, and the ultimate key to social development. This is closer to technological determinism than to Marxism.

It is the relations between men in production which form the economic base or economic structure, determining the characteristic legal, political and ideological forms of each society.

'The production relations of every society form a whole', says Marx. It is the nature of this 'whole' or structure which is the key to the superstructure, consequently no 'element' or part of the superstructure can be explained by reference to some *particular* economic fact or social relation of production, but only on the basis of an analysis of the economic structure as a structure, as a whole. (Needless to say, the 'explanation' of social phenomena directly by reference to technology is even more ludicrous.)

Marxist theory, however, does not involve relating political and ideological manifestations directly to the 'economic base'. Labriola, expanding on the writings of Marx and Engels, expresses this very clearly:

> ... there is no fact which does not recall by its origin the conditions of the underlying economic structure, but there is no fact in history which is not preceded, accompanied and followed by determined forms of consciousness, whether it be superstitious or experimental, ingenuous or reflective, impulsive or self-controlled, fantastic or reasoning. (*Essays on the Materialist Conception of History*, Monthly Review Press, New York, 1966, p. 113)

This attention to the detailed relationships of every specific historical form follows from the Marxist method itself:

> ... we have not to translate into economic categories all the complex manifestations of history, but only to explain in the last analysis (Engels) all the historic facts by means of the underlying economic structure (Marx), which necessitates analysis and reduction and then interlinking and construction. (*Ibid*, p. 111)

The great Marxists have always held fast to this method, and rejected any vulgarization. Lenin, for example, makes characteristic notes on the Russian critic Shulyatikov. Where Shulyatikov writes, 'When dealing with the philosophical system of this or that bourgeois thinker, we are dealing with a picture of the class structure of society', Lenin comments, 'Incorrect!', and calls the 'analysis': 'a vulgarization ... the struggle of the bourgeoisie against feudalism is completely forgotten'. Lenin's complaint is that Shulyatikov presents, 'Instead of a concrete analysis of periods, formations, ideologies — empty phrases about "organisms" and ridiculously strained, absurdly false comparisons. A caricature ...' ('Philosophical Notebooks', *Collected Works*, Vol. 38, pp. 486, 502)

By 'forces of production' Marx does not mean only techniques, or implements, or natural forces harnessed by technique. He places the actual forms of co-operation between men in labour among the forces of production: 'Not only have we here an increase in the productive power of the individual, by means of co-operation, but the creation of a new power, namely, the power of the masses'

Earlier, Marx had expressed himself similarly: 'Of all the instruments of production, the greatest productive power is the revolutionary class itself.' (*The Poverty of Philosophy*, p.146) When Marx writes of 'forces of production' he therefore means the totality of the developed ability of man to confront and transform nature. This consists of all the conquests of man in this field now at his disposal, the cultural heritage of past generations. These forces of production can never exist separately from the property relations into which men enter for their use, but nonetheless the distinction between productive forces and production relations is decisive for Marx's theory. When Marx says that particular forms of class structure are bound up with definite phases of the development of the productive forces, this is a historical, dialectical statement: the further development of production will at a certain point conflict with the property relations.

The production (property) relations do not adapt automatically to necessary changes in the productive forces. They consist of human relations, class interests, and the consciousness of these interests in varying degrees. A struggle between the interests represented in these class or property relations is necessary. Such a struggle originates, develops and unfolds through stages which are not determined directly by the economic base, but according to the laws of the class struggle itself, which has a relative autonomy and requires a developed strategy and tactics based on the interrelations between all these levels.

Before expanding this explanation of the ideological superstructure and the theory of revolution, something must be said about the 'relations of production' which are 'indispensable and independent' of men's wills. In the first place, Marx accords a definite and necessary role to each historically successive mode of production. For the forces of production to develop beyond the restrictions of feudalism, for example, capitalist property relations were necessary. Capitalism required on the one hand the concentration of means of production in a form of ownership which permitted their development and maximum utilization, and on the other hand the reduction of all producers to a state of propertylessness and freedom from all personal, local, traditional ties. All the products of labour, including labour-power itself, which lives in the labourers, must become commodities. Having played the vital role of concentrating in a socialized form the means of production at a level bordering on the possibility of abundance, creating an international division of labour and a proletariat with no future but capitalism's overthrow, the capitalist system of production relations then conflicts with the further necessities of this concentration, socialization and internationalization.

This historical 'necessity' or 'indispensability' of each system of the social relations of production has another aspect. It arises each day for the members of a given society out of the nature of the system itself and not at all out of the wishes or plans of the persons concerned. Far from 'society' or 'social structure' arising out of simple addition of 'unit-acts' by independent individuals, as bourgeois sociology teaches, each of these acts arises out of a pre-existing economic structure born out of necessity at a given stage of historical development. This necessity is reinforced, during and then 'beyond' its time by the political state apparatus and the ideological superstructure which grew up on its base, constantly reproducing assumptions of its normality and inevitability.

For production to take place, and humanity to survive, labour must be joined to the means of production. But under capitalism, labour-power can confront the means of production each day only in the form of wage-labour which has first entered into a contract with the capitalist owner of these means of production. There are no other means of production but those owned as capital, and the labourer has no other access to these means. The secret of these bourgeois relations of production is not to be found in this 'free contract' of the sale of labour-power for wages, which is only the imprint placed upon it as part of the legal and ideological superstructure, but in the antagonism of the two main classes, capitalists and proletarians.

The position of men in these definite relations of production is the starting point of all other forms of social interaction. Even at the level of individual choice, the range and nature of this choice is defined by these basic relations, although their effect is mediated by other social institutions and their history in forming consciousness. To elevate the 'needs' and 'choices' of the consumers of products to the level of an explanatory factor for the economic system, as 'economists' have done over two centuries, is to turn the actual process on its head, says Marx:

> True, the worker who buys potatoes and the kept woman who buys lace both follow their respective judgements. But the difference in their judgements is explained by the difference in the positions which they occupy in the world, and which themselves are the product of social organization. (*The Poverty of Philosophy*, p.37)

Marx adds that in any case many of the 'needs' which are brought to the market are needs not of individual consumers, but of *production* itself, and the latter is determined in its demands by factors beyond the immediate 'judgement' of the individual capitalist. How and what he chooses is decided by his needs *as an owner of capital*, a member of a definite class, etc. Underlying the world of exchange of products, where individuals, proceeding from their rights and freedom of contract, decide what to exchange, is the really determining structure:

> In principle there is no exchange of products — but there is the exchange of the labour which co-operated in production. The mode of exchange of products depends upon the mode of exchange of the productive forces. In general, the form of exchange of products correspond to the form of production. Change the latter, and the former will see change in consequence. Thus in the history of society we see that the mode of exchanging products is regulated by the mode of producing them. Individual exchange corresponds also to a definite mode of production which itself corresponds to class antagonism. There is thus no individual exchange without the antagonism of classes ...(*Ibid.*)

We shall see below that Engels' comments in his later correspondence are not a 'revision' of the 'basis-superstructure' hypothesis here put forward by Marx, as some critics have claimed, but only a warning against its mechanical application, which might arise from an uncritical view of the necessity in the early days of emphasizing the primacy of the economic structure. Meanwhile we return to the 1859 text; Marx continues:

> At a certain stage of their development, the material forces of production in society come into conflict with the existing relations of production, or — what is but a legal expression for the same thing — with the property relations within which they have been at work before.

> From forms of development of the forces of production, these relations turn into their fetters. Then begins an epoch of social revolution. With the change of the economic foundations the entire immense superstructure is more or less rapidly transformed. In considering such transformations a distinction should always be made between the material transformation of the economic conditions of production, which can be determined with the precision of natural science, and the legal, political, religious, aesthetic or philosophic — in short, ideological forms in which men become conscious of this conflict and fight it out.

> Just as our opinion of an individual is not based on what he thinks of himself, so can we not judge of such a period of transformation by its own consciousness; on the contrary this consciousness must be explained rather from the contradictions of material life, from the existing conflict between the social forces of production and the relations of production. No social order ever disappears before all the productive forces for which there is room in it have been developed; and the new higher relations of production never appear before the material conditions of their existence

have matured in the womb of the old society itself. Therefore, mankind always sets itself only such tasks as it can solve; since, looking at the matter more closely, we will always find that the task itself only arises when the material conditions necessary for its solution already exist or are at least in the process of formation.

This passage needs little interpretation, and we have already anticipated much of the argument, in explaining the concepts of 'social relations of production' and 'economic structure'. The transition from one socio-economic system to another is not a mechanical process, but is 'fought out' by men on the basis of economic contradictions. This fight is between classes and sections of classes whose consciousness in the struggle is not a direct reflection of the economic conditions from which the struggle flows, but is mediated through the political and ideological forms already grown up at an earlier phase of the old society's development. A very close study of these mediations is necessary, and they can never be established with the same precision as can the 'material' changes in the economic base. Marx is interested in this study not simply as a guide to historical research, but as a guide to working-class action.

The working class's own position required a penetration to the economic roots of its struggle, and a method to comprehend the political and ideological obstacles, the influence of enemy classes, along this path. It was precisely with this in mind that Marx had analysed in such detail the revolutionary events of 1848-1850. In these writings (*The Class Struggles in France 1848-1850, The 18th Brumaire of Louis Bonaparte, Revolution and Counter Revolution in Germany.*) Marx demonstrates that the ideological forms and political expressions of class interests are not 'mere appearance', but the necessary forms in which the struggle is fought out, and that the working class, with the help of its Marxist theorists, must analyse, grasp and overcome these expressions.

Thus, when the bourgeois republicans of 1848 conceived of their actions and aims on the model of the Great Revolution of 1789, they were summoning up the experience of their class, through its characteristic ideological distortions of the whole cultural heritage and not through scientific analysis, the consciousness and the passions necessary to fit them for a political revolution. Similarly their predecessors in 1789 itself had in thought garbed themselves in the robes of the orators of the Roman Republic. The sordidness of the bourgeois conditions which were to be the real consequences of their actions was altogether too prosaic to inspire either the efforts of these bourgeois themselves or the heroic mass initiatives of the *sans-culottes* of Paris and the peasants who formed the Republican and Napoleonic armies.

The famous opening paragraphs of Marx's *The 18th Brumaire of Louis Bonaparte* elaborate this theme with that striking unity of form and content for which Marx always strove in his writing:

> . . . unheroic as bourgeois society is, it nevertheless took heroism, sacrifice, terror, civil war and battles of peoples to bring it into being. And in the classically austere traditions of the Roman Republic its gladiators found the ideals and the art forms, the self-deceptions that they needed in order to conceal from themselves the bourgeois limitations of the content of their struggles to keep their enthusiasm on the high plane of the great historical tragedy. Similarly, at another stage of development, a century earlier, Cromwell and the English people had borrowed speech, passions and illusions from the Old Testament for their bourgeois revolution. When the real aim had been achieved, when the bourgeois revolution of English society had been accomplished, Locke supplanted Habakkuk. Thus the awakening of the dead in those revolutions served the purpose of glorifying the new struggles, not of parodying the old; of magnifying the given task in imagination, not of fleeing from its solution in reality; of finding once more the spirit of revolution, not of making its ghost walk about again.

Marx goes on to show that in contrast to 1789 this 'magnifying the given task in the imagination' brought in 1848 only a counter-revolution and a tragic farce, because the epoch of a *new* type of revolution had dawned.

> The social revolution of the 19th century cannot draw its poetry from the past, but only from the future. It cannot begin with itself before it has stripped off all superstition in regard to the past. Earlier revolutions required recollections of past world history in order to drug themselves concerning their own content. In order to arrive at its own content, the revolution of the 19th century must let the dead bury their dead. There the phrase went beyond the content; here the content goes beyond the phrase.

These citations demonstrate what Marx meant by saying it was necessary to explain the consciousness of a revolutionary epoch 'from the contradictions of material life, from the existing conflict between the social forces of production and the relations of production', instead of explaining historical epochs from the consciousness of the participants. At the same time, Marx provides a vivid proof of the historical necessity of this 'appearance' of the social reality in the minds of the participants. They cannot 'fight out' the conflict in the base of society except by struggling through these forms of ideology. The forms are not at all mere deception but the necessary, contradictory forms through which the content develops. And yet it is only now, from the standpoint of the proletariat, a class which must dissolve these illusions, that their illusory character can be understood. Through the struggle for this understanding, as two types of revolution, the bourgeois and the proletarian, interpenetrate in 1848, the working class clarifies and arms itself to overthrow the old society.

When Marx says that 'no social order ever disappears before all the productive forces for which there is room in it have developed,' he is not saying that once these forces have been developed, then the social order disappears as a reflex action. This is made clear in the sentences which follow. For the transition to a new social order to be effected, men must pose great historical tasks for themselves, and develop the means to accomplish them. They can only do this effectively when the 'material conditions' for the new order are maturing in the old and thereby disrupting the old forms of consciousness and throwing the classes into conflict.

The forms of this process cannot be deduced from the contradictions in the economic base nor calculated exactly. They are the results of a struggle at a relatively independent level raised on this economic base and at the same time tracing many of its elements from the cultural deposits of the disappearing epoch, and even of earlier epochs. Far from implying a mechanical transition flowing from the economic contradictions, Marx is in fact indicating the necessary (though not sufficient) conditions under which the necessary mobilization and consciousness of the revolutionary class can be formed. It has been a recurring misunderstanding or distortion of Marxism to conceive of some objective 'economic' collapse of capitalism, which then leaves the historical scene vacant for socialism.

Marx's own words in 1859 are a warning not only against Utopian and adventuristic playing with revolutionary phrases at a stage when capitalism still has much of its course to run — and he and Engels soon corrected their own over-optimism in 1848-1850 — but also against this theory of automatic collapse. It is only through the class struggle, which has its own tempo and logic, and goes through its own phases, that the transition can be prepared and accomplished. If we return, for example, to the 1848 writings we find Marx making precisely such a judgement on the necessity of the experience of the defeats of that year. Only through this experience and the theoretical lessons of it, could the proletariat clarify its own tasks. Thus Marx begins *The Class Struggles in France 1848-1850* as follows:

> With the exception of a few short chapters, every important part of the annals of the revolution from 1848 to 1849 carries the heading: *Defeat of the revolution!*
>
> But what has succumbed in these defeats was not the revolution. It was the pre-revolutionary appendages, results of social relationships, which had not yet come to the point of sharp class antagonisms — persons, illusions, conceptions, projects, from which the revolutionary party before the February Revolution was not free, from which it could be freed, not by the victory of February, but only by a series of defeats.
>
> In a word: revolutionary advance made headway not by immediate tragicomic achievements, but on the contrary by the creation of a powerful united counter-revolution, by the creation of an opponent, by fighting whom the party of revolt first ripened into a real revolutionary party.

The lessons of 1848-1849 could therefore be learned not simply through analytical contemplation, but only by a theory which worked through the actual experiences of the class struggle at that historical turning-point. Here as everywhere Marx's thinking develops as part of the struggle of the working class, as the sharp point of its developing consciousness against its enemies. Once this is grasped, all notion of Marxism as a predeterminism must be discarded, and the 'mystery' of why Marx should advocate revolution if he thought capitalism's collapse inevitable is solved.

The matter was taken up directly by Trotsky in the period immediately following the Russian Revolution and the subsequent Civil War and Wars of Intervention, and his presentation will serve as illustration. Addressing Moscow Communists on the subject of the Third World Congress of the new Third (Communist) International, he said:

> But when the productive forces, when technology become too restricted within an old framework, say that of slavery, or feudal or bourgeois society, and when a change of social forms becomes necessary for the further growth of mankind's power, then this is not accomplished automatically, like the sun rises and sets, but must be accomplished through human beings, through the struggle of human beings welded into classes. To replace a social class, governing an old society that has turned reactionary, must come a new social class which possesses the programme for a new social order meeting the needs for the development of productive forces, and which is prepared to realize this programme in life. But it by no means always happens when a given social system has outlived itself, i.e.,

has turned reactionary, that a new class appears, conscious enough, organized enough and powerful enough to cast down life's old masters and pave the way for new social relations. No, this does not at all always happen. On the contrary, more than once, it has happened in history that an old society exhausted itself, for example, the ancient slave society of Rome — and preceding it there were the ancient Asian civilizations whose foundation of slavery opened up no room for the development of productive forces. But within this outlived society there existed no new class strong enough to overthrow the slaveholders and institute a new, feudal system, because the feudal system was, compared to slavery, a step forward. In its turn, within the feudal system there was not always to be found in the hour of need a new class, the bourgeoisie, to overthrow the feudalists and to open the road for historical development. It has more than once happened in history that a given society, a given nation or people, or a tribe, or several tribes and nations, living under similar historical conditions, have run up against the impossibility of developing any further on a given economic foundation — slavery or feudalism — but inasmuch as no new class existed among them capable of leading them out to the main highway, they simply fell apart. The given civilization, the given state, the given society has disintegrated. Mankind has thus not always moved upwards from below in a steady, rising curve. No, there have been prolonged periods of stagnation and there have been regressions into barbarism. Societies rose upwards, attained certain levels, but were unable to maintain themselves upon these heights. Mankind does not remain standing in one place, owing to class and national struggles its equilibrium is unstable; a society that is unable to move forward, falls back, and if no class exists to lift it higher, this society begins to fall apart, opening the road to barbarism. (*First Five Years of the Communist International*, New Park Publications, Volume Two, pp.2-3)

Trotsky's remarks bring home the other corollary of Marx's emphasis on class struggle and revolutionary consciousness. History is not a straight line, with every economic structure preparing its adequate consciousness, efficiently discarding everything that is irrelevant or obstructive. Marx held fast to his early insistence that 'history does nothing', 'it is real living men', in their given social relations, who fight out these historical struggles; and they do it not with a picture in their minds of the overall structure of their historical tasks, but each according to the developed division of labour and consciousness in his own sphere of activity. And this unevenness directly affects the struggle of the working class and the socialist revolution.

Without here going into the actual development of this unevenness in the epoch of wars and revolutions which began in 1914 and is still in process, Trotsky's summary will suffice for the general principle involved:

> The gist of the matter lies in this, that the different aspects of the historical process — economics, politics, the state, the growth of the working class — do not develop simultaneously along parallel lines. The working class does not grow parallel, point for point, with the growth of the productive forces, while the bourgeoisie does not decay nor wither away parallel with the growth and strengthening of the proletariat.

We shall see, when considering the problems dealt with in *Capital*, that Marx did not separate his 'economic' analysis from this life-and-death struggle, any more than economic contradictions and class struggle were separate in history. Outlining his plans for the work to Engels, he says he will proceed finally to 'the class struggle, in which the whole thing is smashed up.'

When, therefore, Marx completes his summary of the materialist conception of history with a series of 'epochs', he is giving only a very general outline and not a fixed scheme:

> In broad outlines we can designate the Asiatic, the ancient, the feudal and the modern bourgeois modes of production as so many epochs in the progress of the economic formation of society. The bourgeois relations of production are the last antagonistic form of the social process of production — antagonistic not in the sense of individual antagonism, but of one arising from the social conditions of life of the individuals; at the same time the productive forces developing in the womb of bourgeois society create the material conditions for the solution of that antagonism. This social formation constitutes, therefore, the closing chapter of the pre-historic stage of human society.

These 'broad outlines' are suggested on the basis of wide-ranging researches by Marx into *Pre-Capitalist Economic Formations*. His notes on these earlier social forms take up a considerable part of the *Grundrisse* or manuscript notes preparatory for the *Critique of Political Economy* and *Capital*.

In later years (1880), Marx read enthusiastically Lewis Henry Morgan's *Ancient Society*, and his notes on this book led Engels to write *The Origin of the Family, Private Property and the State*. Marx undoubtedly considered that Morgan's researches, and above all the discovery of the gentile (clan) form of organization as a universal stage of pre-civilized societies, necessitated a precision and re-working of his own earlier ideas on the subject of society's early history.

Those who seek in Marx a single, unchanging conception of the stages of social development will be disappointed. He responded to the beginnings of anthropological and archaeological research in a scientific way, and any Marxist working in this field today will need to take into account the enormous growth of our knowledge of prehistory and the history of the ancient world which has been gained since Marx and Engels died.

Engels on 'base and superstructure'

Engels' letters on historical materialism, written between 1890 and 1894, are invaluable as warnings against the recurrent oversimplification or vulgarization of the theory; at the same time they contain important precisions of some points. Seen against the background of the material brought together in the preceding pages of this book, Engels' letter cannot by any stretch of imagination be construed as a movement away from the theories formulated by Marx and himself.

Writing to Conrad Schmidt (August 5, 1890) Engels refers to the use of 'materialistic' as a mere label to dispose of historical problems: 'But our conception of history is above all a guide to study, not a lever for construction after the manner of the Hegelians. All history must be studied afresh, the conditions of existence of the different formations of society must be individually examined before the attempt is made to deduce from them the political, legal, aesthetic, philosophical, religious, etc., notions corresponding to them.'

Engels then says that 'economic history is still in its cradle', and nearly four years later he writes, 'In Germany the greatest hindrance to correct understanding is the irresponsible neglect by literature of economic history' (Letter to Starkenburg, January 25, 1894). These remarks are a necessary warning not only to Engels' younger contemporaries, but also to many of their successors, who think that 'Marxism' is a master-key to unlock all doors, at the same time excusing its adherents from hard work.

The same point is made for a different purpose in Engels' next letter: 'Unfortunately it happens only too often that people think they have fully understood a theory and can apply it without more ado from the moment they have mastered its main principles, and these even not always correctly. I cannot exempt many of the more recent 'Marxists' from this reproach, for the most wonderful rubbish has been produced from this quarter too.' (Engels to Joseph Bloch, September 21, 1890).

In this case Engels' strictures are prompted by the question: 'How do Marx and Engels understand the basic principle of the materialist conception of history? . . . is the determining factor in the final analysis *only* production and reproduction in real life, or is this only the basis for all other relations, which themselves exert a further influence?' Engels' reply has become classical:

> According to the materialist conception of history the determining element in history is *ultimately* the production and reproduction in real life. More than that neither Marx nor I have ever asserted. If therefore somebody twists this into the statement that the economic element is the *only* determining one, he transforms it into a meaningless, abstract and absurd phrase. The economic situation is the basis, but the various elements of the superstructure — political forms of the class struggle and its consequences, constitutions established by the victorious class after a successful battle, etc. — forms of law — and then even the reflexes of all these actual struggles in the brains of the combatants: political, legal, philosophical theories, religious ideas and their further development into systems of dogma — also exercise their influence upon the course of the historical struggles and in many cases preponderate in determining their *form*. There is an interaction of all these elements, in which, amid all the endless *host* of accidents (i.e., of things and events whose inner connection is so remote or so impossible to prove that we regard it as absent and can neglect it), the economic movement finally asserts itself as necessary. Otherwise the application of the theory to any period of history one chose would be easier than the solution of a simple equation of the first degree. (*Ibid.*)

As Engels notes later in the letter, these principles of method, here re-asserted in 1890, may be seen in use by studying the original sources: 'Marx hardly wrote anything in which it (historical materialism) did not play a part. *The 18th Brumaire of Louis Bonaparte* is a most excellent example of its application. There are also many allusions in *Capital*.'

He then refers the reader to his own *Anti-Dühring* and *Ludwig Feuerbach*, and concludes that he and Marx must share the blame for the oversimplified conclusions of some of their followers:

> We had to emphasise this main principle in opposition to our adversaries, who denied it, and we had not always the time, the place or the opportunity to allow the other elements involved in the interaction to come into their rights. *But when it was a case of presenting a section of history, that is, of a*

practical application, the thing was different and there no error was possible. (my emphasis — C.S.)

The way in which this interaction takes place, with 'superstructural' elements deciding the *form* in which the content is expressed, is taken up in detail in the remaining letters:

> On the whole, the economic movement gets its way, but it has also to suffer reactions from the political movement *which it established and endowed with relative independence itself* . . . Just as the movement of the industrial market is, in the main and with the reservations already indicated, reflected in the money market and, of course, in inverted form, so the struggle between the classes already existing and already in conflict with one another is reflected in the struggle between government and opposition, but also in inverted form, no longer directly but indirectly, not as a class struggle but as a fight for political principles, and so distorted that it has taken us thousands of years to get behind it again. (My emphasis — C.S. Engels to C. Schmidt, October 27, 1890).

Engels then outlines the development of law in relation to economic conditions, from which he draws conclusions of general validity for the way the superstructure determines the *form* in which the economic content is expressed. As he has said earlier, 'The thing is easier to grasp from the point of view of the division of labour':

> Thus to a great extent the course of the 'development of law' only consists: first in the attempt to do away with the contradictions arising from the direct translation of economic relations into legal principles, and to establish a harmonious system of law, and then in the repeated breaches made in this system by the influence and pressure of further economic development, which involves it in further contradictions . . .
>
> The reflection of economic relations as legal principles is necessarily also a topsy turvy one; it happens without the person who is acting being conscious of it; the jurist imagines he is operating with *a priori* principles, whereas they are really only economic reflexes; so everything is upside down. And it seems to me obvious that this inversion, which, so long as it remains unrecognized, forms what we call *ideological conception,* reacts in its turn upon the economic basis and may, within certain limits, modify it. *(Ibid).*

After pointing out that the development of this 'ideological conception' is more complex in 'the realms of ideology which soar still higher in the air, religion, philosophy, etc.', Engels concludes:

> I consider the ultimate supremacy of economic development established in these spheres too, but it comes to pass within conditions imposed by the particular sphere itself: in philosophy, for instance, through the operation

of economic influences (which again generally act under political, etc. disguises) upon the existing philosophical material handed down by predecessors. Here economy creates nothing absolutely new (*a novo*), but it determines the way in which the existing material of thought is altered and further developed, and that too for the most part indirectly, for it is the political, legal and moral reflexes which exercise the greatest direct influence upon philosophy.

The 18th Brumaire of Louis Bonaparte and *Capital*, says Engels, are sufficient answer to those who say that Marxism denies any role to the political and ideological reflexes of economic development. 'What these gentlemen lack' he says, 'is dialectic. They never see anything but here cause and there effect . . .Hegel has never existed for them'. This point is repeated in a little more detail in Engels' letter to Franz Mehring (July 14, 1893), and all the points made above are repeated in the letter to Heinz Starkenburg (January 25, 1894), though it must be noted that Engels specifically requested that its formulations should be taken in their general signification and not as finished in any way for publication.

These letters, written in the 1890s, have great value as expositions of the Marxist theory of the relation between base and superstructure, but they have the added importance of showing that Engels considered his own and Marx' life's work as constituting a coherent whole, from their critical study of the Hegelian dialectic to their analysis of the class struggle in which they participated.

III
The materialist conception of history: part two

Marx and 'progress'

Marx considered capitalism to be 'the last antagonistic form of the social process of production', because within it the productive forces develop to an extent where potentially mankind could have an abundance of material products. But this development of the forces of production as such was bound up with the necessary change in man himself, considered as 'the sum of all his social relations'. The working class's position in capitalist production is such that it does not have a 'mode of appropriation' or mode of exploitation of its own to realize, as the bourgeoisie had in its struggle against feudalism. Its historical role is to eliminate private property in the means of production in conformity with the very 'socialization' of production forced by the scale of production resulting from capitalist competition and accumulation.

The working class is a great oppressed majority. Its revolutionary interests cannot be the exploitation of another section of society, but only the planned organization of production for use. This is why Marx writes of the end of 'prehistory' when capitalism is superseded by socialism. Here Marx's dialectic is at its most pregnant. Where capitalism represents the acme of 'alienation', of a situation where man's products take on a life independent of him and stand over and against him as alien powers, it also 'universalizes' all these powers, concentrates them as the accumulated conquests of man as social producer, and presents him with the task of mastering them with no local or petty restrictions, but entirely through the comprehension and exercise of his real powers.

In his early writings Marx had striven to define the 'alienation' talked about by Hegel in terms of men's real social relations. In the *Grundrisse* (manuscript notes for *Capital*), he returns to the theme, having enriched it with his historical researches and able to show why the capitalist epoch's particular character has brought the question forward so imperatively, at the same time producing the source of its solution, capitalism's gravedigger, the proletariat. Marx compares this stage of development with the ancient world:

> Thus the ancient conception, in which man always appears (in however narrowly national, religious or political a definition) as the aim of production, seems very much more exalted than the modern world, in which production is the aim of man and wealth the aim of production. In fact, however, when the narrow bourgeois form has been peeled away, what is wealth, if not the universality of needs, capacities, enjoyments, productive powers, etc., of individuals, produced in universal exchanges? What, if not the full development of human control over the forces of nature — those of his own nature as well as those of so-called 'nature'? What, if not the absolute elaboration of his creative dispositions, without any preconditions other than antecedent historical evolution which makes the totality of this evolution, i.e. the evolution of all human powers as such, unmeasured by any previously established yardstick — an end in itself? What is this, if not a situation where man does not reproduce himself in any determined form, but produces his totality? Where he does not seek to remain something formed by the past, but is in the absolute movement of becoming? In bourgeois political economy — and in the epoch of production to which it corresponds — this complete elaboration of what lies within man, appears as the total alienation, and the destruction of all fixed, one-sided purposes as the sacrifice of the end in itself to a wholly external compulsion. Hence in one way the childlike world of the ancients appears to be superior; and this is so, in so far as we seek for closed shape, form and established limitation. The ancients provide a narrow satisfaction, whereas the modern world leaves us unsatisfied or, when it appears to be satisfied with itself, is vulgar and mean. (*Pre-Capitalist Economic Formations*, Lawrence and Wishart, 1964, pp. 84-85)

Marx's view, here outlined, of the universal gains for mankind which are represented in the achievements of the productive forces under capitalism, is related to a general concept of progress in his theoretical outlook, and is not just a passing thought. Written in 1858, it carries forward into a historical and thereby more concrete dimension the humanism embodied in his theory of alienation of the early 1840s. He was to go further in *Capital*, there making precise the way in which men's social relations are transmuted and represented by the value-form as the properties (values) of things on the market (commodity fetishism and the other characteristic ideological forms of capitalism). Further, his purpose in *Capital* is to demonstrate that within the process of reproduction of these social forms there is also necessarily produced the class force which will disrupt it or 'smash it up'.

So, while Marx did consider that the historical development of man's own productive forces was the basis of a real human progress, he saw this progress not as a smooth evolution and not as predetermined or conforming to some 'purpose'. Instead, he saw a series of revolutionary leaps in history, made necessary by the inertia of the social systems established on the previously existing level of development of productive forces. The cumulative and progressive nature of historical development is especially emphasized in Trotsky's work, devoted as it is to the turbulent history of the 20th century, 'the epoch of wars and revolutions' (Lenin). Without having had access to these notes written by Marx in the 1850s, Trotsky himself pointed out the same special contribution of capitalism to human progress as did Marx. Rejecting the theory that backward Russia must repeat the sequence of historical development passed through by the advanced countries, he writes:

> The theory of the repetition of historic cycles — Vico and his more recent followers — rests upon an observation of orbits of old pre-capitalist cultures, and in part upon the first experiments of capitalist development. A certain repetition of cultural stages in ever new settlements was in fact bound up with the provincial and episodic character of that whole process. Capitalism means, however, an overcoming of those conditions. *It prepares and in a certain sense realizes the universality and permanence of man's development.* By this a repetition of the forms of development of different nations is ruled out. (My emphasis — C.S.) (*The History of the Russian Revolution,* Gollancz, London, 1936, p. 26.)

At the other end of the historical scale — the emergence of humanity from barbarism to civilization — we can expect to find a great variety and complexity of development, but for very different reasons. Whereas modern productive forces and the conquests of science reduce geographical variations to incidental matters affecting only the form of progress, pre-civilized peoples were, on the contrary, exceedingly strictly limited to a very delicate adjustment to the immediate possibilities in their natural environment. Their low productive level inhibited any transgression of these limits and placed a high premium on tradition and conservatism. This, together with the limited range of contact *between* societies (the latter is also in essence a consequence of the backwardness of productive forces: means of communication are a part of these), as well as the absence of a surplus product to necessitate external contacts, contributes to a situation where war and conquest are an engine of change and the principal method of contact between the separate societies.

In Marx's day, knowledge of these pre-civilized societies and of early civilizations was meagre in comparison with present knowledge, and in the course of his life Marx changed his formulations of the problem of defining the early stages of social evolution. Morgan's researches enabled Marx to clarify some of the obscurities of his formulations in the *Grundrisse* but they do not invalidate his main point; that the different early civilizations took their form from the different ways in which the original communal property broke up. The early civilizations based on large-scale irrigation works exemplified in the most developed form that particular mode of transition from tribal community which, while it broke down many of the functions of the old descent organizations, at the same time inhibited the growth of that major source of historical development, private property in land.

The great civilizations based on the irrigation of flood valleys (on the Nile, Tigris and Euphrates) therefore suffered the historical fate of providing a stimulus and eventually a source of plunder for peoples whose development from tribal organization took another path, such as the Phoenicians, the Greeks and the Romans. There is thus a certain sense, from the 'world-historical' point of view, in which 'oriental despotism', while not itself developing into a higher form of civilization, was a necessary element in the birth of those ancient Mediterranean cultures which formed the seed-bed of European feudalism and capitalism. The work of many prehistorians, and particularly of V. Gordon Childe,* has documented this process in great detail.

The same 'unevenness', and the process by which a particular society may meet its historical doom, its conquests being carried forward only by others which in many respects are more backward, are characteristic of later phases too. Thus, the Roman Empire, while preparing the elements of the next, feudal, period in the development of the productive forces, could itself neither develop these any further nor produce from within itself a class which could overthrow the now parasitic slave-imperial order. At another level, the first European

---

* *New Light on the Most Ancient East, What Happened in History*, and especially, *The Pre-history of European Societies*.

powers to develop capitalism soon found themselves at a disadvantage with others, originally more 'backward', whose very backwardness left the field open for a more dynamic development. Eventually we find backward nations drawn into the maelstrom of the present period of highly-developed and over-ripe capitalism already pregnant with the socialist revolution. It is this particular level of the 'law of uneven development' which is grasped in Lenin's *Imperialism* and Trotsky's *Permanent Revolution*.

Any mechanical and vulgar appreciation of Marx's theory of social development as a series of set stages for each separate society could not explain the present historical development of, say, Egypt. Here was one of those areas which 'overdeveloped' in the transition from barbarism to civilization, then fell victim to the newer and more vigorous Mediterranean powers which built upon Egypt's (and Mesopotamia's) own advances. Egypt now finds itself drawn back into world history not at all through the highly-specialized exploitation of its own immediate resources (the Nile, domesticable grains suitable for food, etc.) but through an opposite process. The internal development of other 'world-historical' powers impels them to expand all over the globe, and to break up all existing, archaic social relations first through trade and then the export of capital. Society in Egypt develops now as part of this imperialism in crisis.

Hegel thus comes into his own, after the fashion indicated by Marx, by being stood on his head! Hegel wrote his *Logic* and *Philosophy of History* as a celebration of the achievements of the 'absolute spirit' which had its way with men and events even when their intentions and actions took them in 'their own' direction. This 'cunning of reason' was taken by Marx to be the process of man himself transforming the world through his social production, subduing nature to his will through an accumulating knowledge of the laws of nature and development of the productive forces, and adapting his social relations in a series of titanic struggles to this process: 'The labourer . . . makes use of the mechanical, physical, and chemical properties of some substances in order to make other substances subservient to his aims'. (*Capital*, Vol. I, p. 158) Marx then refers directly to the famous passage in Hegel's *Encyclopaedia*:

> Reason is just as cunning as she is powerful. Her cunning consists principally in her mediating activity, which, by causing objects to act and react on each other in accordance with their own nature, in this way, without any direct interference in the process, carries out reason's intentions.

When Hegel examined world history, he produced a great deal of highly speculative systematization instead of scientific investigation, but at the same time he expressed an idea of genius. He recognized that certain civilizations might disappear after only a short life, everything they produced having been broken and plundered by barbarians, and yet, considered as moments of world history, the contributions of such cultures can be seen very differently.

In these very general remarks, we have in fact thrown together different types of this historical unevenness; in some cases we are referring to the transitions between vast historical epochs; in others to different stages in the development of the same socio-economic order, capitalism. In each case, the task of the investigator is to master the existing material on the subject and to carry out his own research, and on no account to seize upon 'the law of uneven and combined development' as a master-key to any and every historical problem.

Trotsky's *History of the Russian Revolution* is, after *Capital*, perhaps the most ambitious and successful application of the theory of historical materialism, bringing to bear particularly those aspects of the theory which were necessary to explain the processes resulting from a backward country's rough entry on to the scene of late capitalist development and the proletarian revolution. It should be said, of course, that this was not a seeking for theoretical explanations 'after the fact'. Trotsky and others (Parvus, Luxemburg, Kautsky, and even Marx himself) had indicated with some precision why this backward country could be expected to provide the prior impetus to, or first break-through of, the socialist revolution (see especially Trotsky's *Results and Prospects*, in *The Permanent Revolution*, New Park Publications 1965).

The 'Asiatic mode of production'

It is the work of specialist historians to generalize the knowledge gained since Marx's day of those societies which he classed under the 'Asiatic mode of production'. When he listed this along with the 'ancient [presumably slave], feudal, and capitalist' modes of production, he was certainly indicating it as a type of society which for definite reasons has preserved a character distinct from others.

His notes in the *Grundrisse* (*Precapitalist Economic Formations*) make it perfectly clear that he considered that the special social characteristics consequent on the exigencies of large-scale irrigation and centralized public works in the great flood-valleys produced a distinct and relatively static form of economy and political system. It is no longer possible to maintain, as did many Marxists, that the term 'Asiatic' in this formulation can be taken simply to mean the equivalent of primitive communism. Certainly Marx had written earlier (1852-1853) that the characteristic feature of Oriental societies was the absence of private property in land, as contrasted with the power and wealth of the despots. But by the end of the 1850s, after very serious study, Marx was certainly classing 'Oriental' or 'Asiatic' society as one of the forms of slow break-up of communal property. Its distinguishing feature, he now thought, was the self-sufficient and static character, based on common ownership, of the economic communities composing it, providing a uniform, undifferentiated base (without any internal impetus to integration) for the overriding despot. He had made a similar analysis of the peasantry as the social basis for Bonapartist dictatorship in modern European society, even calling the peasantry 'the class which represents barbarism within civilization'. (*The 18th Brumaire of Louis Bonaparte.*)

As an example of the tortuous paths of the development of Marxism, and even of the discovery of Marx's own meaning, the fate of this very concept 'the Asiatic mode of production' is of great interest. In the late 1920s, a bitter controversy developed in the USSR, the eventual result of which was to 'abolish' the concept of the Asiatic mode of production. (Karl Wittfogel has given some account of this in his *Oriental Despotism*, Yale University Press, 1957, but only in so far as it supports his own eccentric view that the whole 'plot' began with Marx himself, who changed his mind about Oriental Despotism because it gave aid and comfort to his anarchist opponent, Bakunin!).

Certain features of this controversy are noted here as examples of the relation between historical theories (including Marxism, though in its own specific way) and the social reality from which they spring, rather than as a commentary on the nature of 'Asiatic' society. As already indicated, the latter is a specialist task of another kind; but when it is done, it will need to take into account the dimension of the history of the theory itself, to which we give some preliminary pointers here. Stalin's *Dialectical and Historical Materialism*, originally published in millions of copies as Chapter IV of the *Short History of the Communist Party of the Soviet Union (Bolsheviks): Short Course*, (Foreign Languages Publishing House, Moscow, 1938), was for many years the accepted authority on its subject in the 'official' Communist movement.

Quite apart from its dogmatic and metaphysical distortion of Marx's work, what especially strikes the reader is Stalin's manner of quoting Marx's most famous text on historical materialism, the 'Preface' to the *Contribution to the Critique of Political Economy*. The whole summary made by Marx is quoted, until it stops short before the sentence: 'In broad outlines we can designate the Asiatic, the ancient, the feudal, and the modern bourgeois mode of production. . . '

This glaring omission was not an oversight or an exception. Seven years before, the Soviet academician M. Godes had pronounced sentence on the concept of 'the Asiatic mode of production': 'This theory, politically harmful, methodologically incorrect, must be done away with.' Thirteen years after the 1938 Stalin publication, the eminent Soviet historian E. A. Kosminsky, asked for information on this matter by a group of British Marxists working on oriental studies, wrote in reply:

> . . . At any rate the history of mankind does not know any 'Asiatic mode of production' distinct from the principal modes of production as they are stated, for instance, by Stalin in the fourth chapter of the *History of the Communist Party* . . . It is quite fruitless to examine the printed materials touching these discussions; the names mentioned in the latter belong to the long-forgotten dilettantes of 'Pokrovsky's School' and opinions are quite irrelevant for a modern Marxist student. (*The Asiatic Mode of Production*, Discussion by the Society of Marxist Orientalists, State Social-Economic Publishing House, Moscow 1951)

In point of fact, the 'abolition' of the concept of the Asiatic mode of production was above all else a political task undertaken as part of the consolidation of Stalin's faction in the Soviet Communist Party, the Third International and the Soviet State. Quite explicitly, the concept of the Asiatic mode was attacked as a deviation from Marxism specifically linked to the political line of Stalin's opponents on the question of the revolution in China, where the crushing of the Communists by Chiang Kai-shek had become a crucial international question for the struggle between Stalin and the Left Opposition.

Godes, in the 1931 Leningrad discussion, attacks Lominadze, for example:

> Lominadze, in connection with the Canton commune [a political adventure in 1927 under Stalin's direction which led to disaster — C.S.] gave a Trotskyite viewpoint, depicting the tasks of the revolution as the tasks of a

socialist revolution. It is clear that the denial of feudalism in China, or the evasion of it, always led to political mistakes of just such a Trotskyite nature. (*Ibid*).

More generally, Godes says:

> Here I only want to point out that I do not belong to the number of those who are ready to include their opponents among the Trotskyites for the sake of a simple recognition of the Asiatic mode of production, but for me each theory is important not for what the author's own opinion of it is, but for where this theory leads, what deductions inescapably flow from it when applied to the contemporary East. The theory of the Asiatic mode of production not only perverts Marxism's methodology in radical questions of history, but is also politically harmful as a theory which obscures the question of the remnants of feudalism in the contemporary East. (*Ibid.*)

Concluding his opening report, Godes describes the concept of the Asiatic mode as 'a fertile theoretical base for Trotskyism', and says of the participants in the discussion:

> ... It will be better if they do not limit themselves to a bashful and silent rejection of the application of their methodology to contemporary problems, but make all the proper conclusions of the fact that a theory which ceases to serve the revolution, which is fruitless in application to the present time, should be thrown aside ...(*Ibid.*)

In the course of his 'argument' Godes performs some extraordinary contortions in order to make the current policies of Stalin 'consistent' with earlier statements of the Communist International in which the 'Asiatic mode' was specifically mentioned. Of course it was a travesty to identify the Left Opposition's standpoint on China with an adherence to 'the Asiatic mode'. There was a more general and less explicit sense in which the dominant Stalinist group in the Soviet Union and the Communist International required a rigid unilinearist theory (i.e. a theory of one set of stages through which all societies pass), and could not countenance anything which suggested a more dialectical view. Stalin's particular ideological innovation was the theory of 'socialism in a single country'. From late 1924 onwards Stalin needed to 'prove' that such a theory was consistent with Marxism, even though it had not hitherto been deduced from it. A unilinearist conception, whereby every nation goes through a similar series of inevitable stages, with 'national peculiarities taken into account', etc., was admirably suited to such a perspective. Thus Stalin wrote in 1930:

'... the foundations of the activity of every Communist Party ...on which it must base itself, are the *general features* of capitalism, which are essentially the *same for all countries*, but not the specific features of *one* country. It is precisely on *this* that the internationalism of the Communist Parties rests. The specific features are merely supplementary to the general features.' (*Bolshevik* magazine, No. 1, cited by Trotsky in the Preface to the American Edition of *Permanent Revolution*.)

In point of fact, the internationalism of Marxism had and has a quite *opposite basis,* i.e. capitalism as an international system. On this basis, the 'peculiarities' are not 'merely supplementary to the general features', as Stalin puts it, but specifically developed combinations of the forces at work internationally, concentrating these developments in particular ways which, as Trotsky points out, may be decisive for the strategy of a whole period of years, as indeed in the Russian Revolution. It was this ideological need of Stalin and his bureaucracy to legitimize a 'national' socialism which led to the characteristic distortion of historical materialism in the Stalin period.

This whole trend was, of course, overlaid with the ultra-dogmatism characteristic of a totalitarian inability to brook the slightest suspicion of unorthodoxy. 'Socialism in a single country' versus 'Permanent Revolution', a theoretical and political controversy which was the reflection of the struggle of real forces over the future of the Russian Revolution, was the direct determinant of the major theoretical issues in Marxism in the whole subsequent period, and is the real key to the 'abolition' of the Asiatic mode of production.

As a result of the political obstacles, as well as the enormity of the task, there remains still to be carried out the task of surveying and analysing the evidence of prehistoric archaeology, particularly of the Near East together with information about Africa and other tribal societies in various stages of transition, all accumulated since the times of Marx and Engels. Marxist scholars, not only in the USSR, have been inhibited from the undertaking of this task by the 'official' or Stalinist domination of Marxist studies. Here we suggest only the very general lines along which the picture of the transition to civilization, presented by Marx and Engels, might be re-stated today.

The first relevant text is *Anti-Dühring* (1877-1878). It should be remembered that in this book Engels is replying specifically to Dühring's arguments about the primary role of 'force' (power) in history, and is concerned above all to demonstrate that even in those cases where the control of force by state power appears to be the predominant factor in history, it is conditioned by its origin as a definite social-economic function, and that in so far as it does not continue to perform this function, it will not survive historically. In this context Engels writes: 'The relationship based on the domination and the subjection . . . arose *in two ways.*' (p. 230) (my emphasis, C.S.)

He goes on to describe first the emergence of definite offices for the exercise of necessary community functions:

> . . . the independence of social functions in relation to society increased with time until it developed into domination over society; what was originally the servant developed gradually, where conditions were favourable, into the lord; . . . this lord, on the basis of different conditions, emerged as an Oriental despot or satrap, the dynast of a Greek tribe, chieftain of a Celtic clan, and so on . . . and finally the separate rulers united into a ruling class. (pp. 204-205)

Wittfogel (*Oriental Despotism*) and others have taken this passage to refer to 'Oriental' societies as an *alternative* form of society to the second development (*private property*) to which Engels next refers. According to Wittfogel, Engels was aware of the origin of social classes in those societies where a governing bureaucracy appropriated the surplus product, as contrasted with the state of affairs where economic differentation occurs first, after which the dominant 'economic' class erects a state power to protect its own interests.

By the time of *The Origin of the Family* (1883), Wittfogel claims, Engels had excluded the first path from his consideration, because of the political embarrassment it could have caused to Marx and himself in their dispute with Bakunin, who was arguing precisely against what he called then 'state socialism' as the source of a new form of exploitation through political monopoly.

Anti-Dühring, says Wittfogel, was a half-way house between the scientific honesty of Marx and Engels in the 1850s and Engels' 'dishonest' concealment in 1884. Quite apart from the fact that he fails to show any reason for the *particular* change between 1878 and 1883 (a difference which is actually accounted for by the fact that Marx read and noted Morgan's *Ancient Society*, the notes from which formed the basis of Engels' later book), the chapter in *Anti-Dühring* itself is not at all what Wittfogel makes it out to be. Engels' text continues: 'But alongside of this development of classes another was also taking place.' By this other development he refers to the dissolution of the commune through the growth of division of labour and private property within it, and the growth of slavery, first by using prisoners of war. Engels' point here against Dühring is that 'force' (the disciplining of slaves through war, into enforced labour) 'instead of controlling the economic order, was on the contrary pressed into the service of the economic order'. Engels does not here outline any development of state power directly out of this slavery, he simply notes its historical significance as the form of inequality and class *necessary* to Hellenic and European civilization, and states: 'Without the slavery of antiquity, no modern socialism.' When Engels summarizes the 'two ways' in which 'relationships based on domination and subjection' arose, he writes:

> In the first place, all political power is originally based on an economic, social function, and increases in proportion as the members of society, through the dissolution of the primitive community, become transformed into private producers, and thus become more and more separated from the administrators of the general functions of society. Secondly, after the political force has made itself independent in relation to society, and has transformed itself from its servant into its master, it can work in two different directions . . . (p. 208)

Wittfogel's distortion is evident. Engels here envisages the 'path' of 'dissolution of the commune' into 'private producers' as one which *must accompany* the differentiation of social functions, in order for the latter to give birth to the state as we know it in class society. He describes the 'Oriental Despotisms' as 'the most barbarous form of state', subsisting in conditions where the ancient communes persist, and thereby limited in their development. The use of the term 'barbarous' is not for purposes of condemnation but of historical judgment: the transition from barbarism to civilization could be anticipated, but not accomplished, along that road: 'It was only where these communities dissolved that the peoples made progress of themselves . . .'. Engels does *not* say, as Wittfogel would have him say, 'that dominance based on socio-administrative function united the "individual ruling persons into a ruling class"' (*Oriental Despotism*, p. 384). What Engels does say in *Anti-Dühring* is: 'It is not necessary for us to examine here how this independence of social functions in relation to society increased with time until it developed into domination over society . . . and how finally the separate individual rulers united into a ruling class.' (pp. 204-205)

We have already seen that, in point of fact, Engels goes on to discuss the 'other' path of class differentiation (private property) as the necessary condition for the crystallization of class relations in such a way that the occupants of those public offices became officers of *the state*.

One could certainly regard Engels' three chapters in *The Origin of the Family* on gens and state among the Greeks, Romans and Germans as the 'examination' which he spoke of as 'not necessary here' in *Anti-Dühring*; and it is by then enriched by the work of Morgan. Engels would not have been able to apply these discoveries in the same way to the Near East because knowledge of the gentile constitution of ancient societies in these areas was not available to him, quite apart from his stated reason of lack of time and space.

Further there is not the slightest doubt that our interpretation of the disputed passage in *Anti-Dühring* is entirely supported by the now readily available Marx manuscripts of the 1850s (*Pre-Capitalist Economic Formations*). There Marx contrasts the capacity for progress of that type of tribal society which produced the city and slavery, with that which became the basis for Oriental Despotism:

> The property of the individual unlike our first case, is here not direct communal property, where the individual is not an owner in separation from the community, but rather its occupier. Circumstances arise in which individual property does not require communal labour for its valorization (e.g. as it does in the irrigation systems of the Orient); the purely primitive character of the tribe may be broken by the movement of history or migration; the tribe may remove from its original place of settlement and occupy *foreign* soil, thus entering substantially new conditions of labour and developing the energies of the individual further. The more such factors operate — and the more the communal character of the tribe therefore appears, and must appear, rather as a negative unity as against the outside world — the more do conditions arise which allow the individual to become a *private proprietor* of land — of a particular plot — whose special cultivation belongs to him and his family. (p. 72)

Marx and Engels were not unilinear evolutionists in the sense of considering that each society moved through or had gone through an identical series of stages. Nor were they 'multilinearists' in the sense of considering that by different paths, separate societies would arrive at similar stages. Nor, finally, did they think that their task was to delineate a series of separate evolutions, each with its own result. That would have been abstract and alien to their method. Marx started from the contemporary capitalist economic structure, characterized by the meeting together of capital and free labour, and he studied pre-capitalist economic formations in order to discover the different forms by which labour had previously been tied to, and then freed from, the land, the basic means of production, as well as the history of money and capital. In so far as a conception of successive stages emerges from the work of Marx and Engels, it is a conception of the stages undergone by human history as a whole. Sometimes one 'society', in realizing its own development, carries this history forward; at other times, another. Unless this integral approach is understood, then the 'answers' given to unilinearism tend to be just as schematic as unilinearism itself.

Stalin's unilinearism might appear to have some support from the famous lecture 'On the State' by Lenin:

> The development of all human societies for thousands of years, in all countries without exception, reveals a general conformity to law, a regularity and consistency; so that at first we had a society without classes — the original patriarchal, primitive society, in which there were no aristocrats; then we had a society based on slavery — a slave-owning society.

Lenin says at the beginning of this lecture that he proposes to take 'a fleeting glance' at the history of the state, and he is addressing students unfamiliar with the literature, as the lecture makes very clear indeed. This lecture was intended as the first of two by Lenin, to be followed by a series of other lectures.

Lenin's first concern here is to insist on the division of society into classes as the foundation of the state. Whatever the variations of state form in a particular type of class society, the essential thing is that it represents the domination of one class over the other. The simplified form of the lecture makes it necessary to correct certain details: The 'original' primitive society was not 'patriarchal'. It is not the case that 'the whole of modern civilized Europe has passed through this stage (slavery)', or that 'the vast majority of peoples of the other parts of the world also passed through this stage.' Nor is it universally the case that 'the division into slave-owners and slaves was the first important class division'.

Further, if Lenin's assertion on a 'conformity to law', 'without exception', is used to justify the view that every single society goes through the same stages, it is misused. The lawfulness, as we have tried to show, is of a different kind, a kind which is of course fully grasped in all Lenin's major writings. In his lecture, Lenin insists that his audience study the original Marxist texts, and particularly Engels' *Origin of the Family, Private Property, and the State*, '... every sentence of which can be accepted with confidence, in the assurance that it has not been said at random, but is based on immense historical and political material'. We know that Lenin was very familiar with Engels' book, and that he certainly could not have considered the 'patriarchal' to be the original form of society. The mistake arises only from brevity and simplification.

Engels' work also leaves no doubt that the 'Germanic' peoples, whose conquest of the Roman Empire brought in the feudal form of society, did not 'pass through' the stage of slavery. They carried civilization beyond the impasse of slavery precisely for this reason. It is therefore not possible to accept 'every word' of Engels' book and 'every word' of Lenin's lecture as it stands. And Lenin would undoubtedly have recognized this and returned to his recommendation of Engels.

It follows that for many peoples like the 'Germanic tribes', the 'division into slave-owners and slaves' was *not* the 'prior important class division'. All the evidence points to feudal-type relations of land-holding and service being, in fact, the most common early form of class society. But European civilization could be founded only when these peoples built upon the conquests of the Roman slave empire.

Where societies emerged from barbarism and set foot on the road to civilization proper, it was through the ability to evolve forms of private property within which the basic productive forces could develop. In general, and over a prolonged period of transition, the communal property of unilineal descent groups in primitive communism obstructed the further development of the productive forces and necessary division of labour in agriculture and in handicrafts. Throughout this long period, antagonisms developed within tribal society, and in many cases the formal rules of marriage, inheritance, and office were adapted in a variety of ways to allow a social differentiation to take place, primarily in the sphere of consumption.

So long as the production of a surplus was relatively irregular and uncertain or insufficiently developed beyond food production to allow for economic differentiation and accumulation of movable property, these differences in the sphere of consumption did not yet break the framework of descent groups and group inheritance, even where they coincided, as they often did, with the allocation of functions of co-ordination and authority, often hereditary, necessary for the community's survival. However, where the division of labour developed in such a way as to require the *internal* differentiation of descent groups, and forms of private property actually disrupted the clan-tribal framework (even if the formal rules remained, and were even used to sustain the new privileges), the state became necessary. (See Engels' *Origin of the Family, Private Property and the State*, 1883, for examples of this process and its different paths.)

Here the occupants of certain offices which had originally developed to *serve* society administratively became rulers *over* society, in the service of those whose interests were to preserve and contain the existing antagonisms, to prevent their expression in ways which would destroy society. In this way the *state* as we know it was born. The historical development from primitive communities along the road which eventually issued in feudalism and capitalism in Europe, and thence throughout the world, thus required a two-fold development. On the one hand, we have the elevation of certain men into social-economic, administrative and ideological functions on behalf of the whole society, from which positions they may appropriate the products of the labour of the rest of society in their capacity as society's representatives. On the other hand, the local communities over which they rule, in the first place continuing with forms of collective property, must go through a process of internal economic differentiation (taking the form of domestic slavery or personal dependence) on the basis of an advance in the division of labour, if a real foundation for economic progress is to be laid.* If the latter does not take place, then the early forms of despotism remain static, and any change in them is brought only from the outside, and then only by an economic effect sufficient to disrupt the local industry and agriculture.

Even where the local communes undergo a certain development of division of labour, with a system of mutual exchange and local self-sufficiency, as in the Indian village commune, and the old descent-group organization decays, so long as private property in land does not develop within the commune then there is no basis for progress, so that: 'the ancient communes, where they have continued to exist, have for thousands of years formed the basis of the most barbarous form of state, oriental despotism, from India to Russia'. (Engels, *Anti-Dühring*)

---

* I leave aside the important question of the role of war and conquest in defining these early class relations. No doubt in some cases the enslavement of prisoners or the imposition of certain forms of clientship or vassalage preceded the actual acceptance of the class division within the same community. In other cases the pressure of population and migration provided the opportunity for defining such relations, with the real or the political claim to hereditary entitlement as their legitimation. Whatever the mechanism it clearly could only operate on this basis of a definite economic development.

Just as the advances made in the flood-valleys of the Nile, the Tigris and the Euphrates were eventually taken forward into the stream of world history only by the originally more backward societies of the Mediterranean, because of the basis there for private property, slavery, the development of iron-working (or rather the wider utilization of its products in agriculture), and trade and commerce, so, at a later date, yet another form of development from the primitive commune, that characterized by the Germans, had to enter the scene of history in order to carry forward the achievements of the Roman Empire.

The social relations characteristic of feudal tenure (serfdom and rent in kind), a form to which European agriculture had to return in order to escape the historical impasse produced by slavery, could only be imposed by the barbarians of the North. This is the interpretation of Marx in the 1850s (*Pre-Capitalist Economic Formations*) just as it is of *Origin of the Family* in 1883. It bears no resemblance to unilinearism or 'multilinearism' and it is surely a framework which facilitates an interpretation of contemporary evidence. It states clearly that social relations of the type we call feudal did not emerge fully-fledged from slavery, but were the product of a particular form of the development and disintegration of tribal society.

It is a form which could now be said to be perhaps the most general of all in the history of society. But only in Europe, on the basis of the previous achievements of a great slave empire, did it develop into a feudal system which produced the nation states and capitalism which eventually were to become universal, through the all-conquering superiority of the capitalist mode of production as such and not through the 'internal development' of each separate society. The development was not 'rational' or planful, and began with the near-destruction of the advances of the ancient empire.

World history shows feudal relations of this type having evolved independently into major civilizations more than once. Japan is the best-known example outside Europe. Russia provides an interesting test. Tsarism certainly had 'Asiatic' or 'Oriental Despotic' features, and Wittfogel tries to use the Russian developments to support his theories. However, from the 10th to the 13th centuries Russia developed a feudal civilization similar in all essentials to that of western Europe.

It is from the Mongol invasion that the 'Asiatic' imprint derives, and for this imprint to be made it was necessary to destroy Russian urban life and to centralize the ownership of land. This is an excellent 'negative' test of Marx's own characterization of Oriental Despotism and the economic basis of both its persistence and its negative relation to social progress. When this social form supervened upon a feudal form, its role was not to provide a fresh opening, but precisely the opposite. Only centuries later, when Russia was brought, through the despotic state in the first place, into organic relationship with capitalist Europe, did Russian society explode into world history as an element of progress, and then only by first having taken to its limit the role of reactionary 'policeman' of Europe.

We stress once again that what is necessary is a detailed investigation of all these social-economic forms and their actual interpenetration at different periods of history. Whilst it is certain that 'blind spots' about the 'Asiatic mode of production' have prevented this, it seems equally true that to expose these blind spots and their origin, and to equip oneself to begin from the richness of uneven and combined development in our own day, is the essential prerequisite (though *only* that) of a scientific approach to the past. This would be a continuation of Marx's own method, for he started out quite consciously from the material *product* of all these past relations in the capitalist system.

The 'oriental despotic' states were nowhere able to transform the levels of production and social organization reached by the ancient communes, whose stability was in fact the precondition of these despotisms. Conquerers succeeded each other, simply plundering, more or less systematically through a bureaucracy, the products of the time-honoured social systems. While the original functionaries of the oriental despotism were raised to their positions because of definite social functions, they did not represent the necessary social relations of a new mode of production. On the contrary, they were the expression of the limit reached by the collective necessities of the old form of society, pushed to its extreme in the particular conditions of organizing large-scale public works for flood-valley irrigation agriculture.

But in so far as they preserved their control over society by bureaucratic repressions and the exaction of tribute, they played the role of preserving those production conditions in the local communes which inhibited the development of economic differentiation; and only the latter could truly (historically) form the basis of class society and the state in the form which carried humanity forward. Where Engels says 'the most barbarous form of state' we should say that it is both state and not state. It brings together all the political and functional elements which are prepared within barbarism for the state power, but even under the exceptional conditions where collective labour on a large scale can provide a surplus product which is the source of considerable privileged wealth, it does not develop to class society and the state in the historical sense. Indeed the very preservation of this state power, because it is not the organ of an essential class in a new mode of production and type of property, works *against* further historical progress within the given society. This 'proto-class' and 'proto-state' is an over-development, so to speak, of elements which must, however, be backed by developments at the heart of production.

The example of Russian history, referred to above, is particularly interesting in this respect. It is clear that the Mongol invaders actually had to destroy the economic development characteristic of feudalism in order to reduce the country to conditions upon which their despotism could subsist. In other words, oriental despotism of one sort or another may rest upon a certain range of types of economy as its base, but it is incompatible with the existence of private property in land and of independent crafts and the urban life which goes with them. Marx himself understood very well that Novgorod, which was not overrun by the Mongols but only later conquered, in 1478, by Ivan III of Muscovy, a state already itself transformed by Mongol subjection, had to be broken before the special developments of Russian absolutism could be completed. Marx notes that the true origins of Muscovy are to be found not in the 'crude glory' of the Kiev era (from the 10th to the 13th centuries) but in the 'bloody filth' of the Mongol yoke. (*Secret Diplomatic History of the 18th Century*)

Here we return to Marx's view of the general human progress involved in the development of production. The 'oriental despot' and his minions must precisely hold back any differentiation within the commune, because it is the manipulation of the separate and internally undifferentiated communes which is the basis of their power. Division of labour and the growth of the surplus product within the commune, however, is the essential process of freeing man from the 'natural' undifferentiated commune and its direct ties to the natural environment. Only by freeing himself from these ties with nature and the primeval commune does man begin the long march to eventually restore communism at a higher level, a truly human and universal level, on the basis of all the conquests of the period of class society.

Marx gives an analogous presentation of the transition from feudalism to capitalism:

> The transition from feudalism to capitalism is two-fold. The producer becomes merchant and capitalist, in contrast to the natural agricultural economy and the guild-bound handicrafts of the medieval urban industries. This is the really revolutionizing path. Or else, the merchant establishes direct sway over production. However much this serves historically as a stepping-stone — witness the English 17th century clothier, who brings the weavers, independent as they are, under his control by selling their wool to them and buying their cloth — it cannot by itself contribute to the overthrow of the old mode of production, but tends rather to preserve and retain it as its pre-condition. (*Capital*, Volume III, p. 324)

Certain of the elements of the next stage of social evolution are thus prepared at one level, but unless they are related to developments along the 'really revolutionizing road', within the basic production relations, they remain quantitative changes. In so far as the more basic development does not take place, then the other development 'tends rather to preserve and maintain' the old mode of production as its pre-condition. This is precisely the role of the 'barbarous' form of state developed out of the necessity of public works and all that went with them in the flood-valleys to ensure the continuation of agriculture.

IV
Classes and class struggle: the economic base

Class as an objective phenomenon

It is often said and written that the class struggle is the core of Marx's theories. Marx himself pronounced on this idea:

> ... no credit is due to me for discovering the existence of classes in modern society, nor yet the struggle between them. Long before me the bourgeois historians have described the historical development of this class struggle and bourgeois economists, the economic anatomy of the classes. What I did that was new was to prove: (1) that the existence of classes is only bound up with particular historic phases in the development of production; (2) that the class struggle necessarily leads to the *dictatorship of the proletariat;* (3) that this dictatorship itself only constitutes the transition to the abolition of *all classes* and to a classless society ...(Marx, letter to Weydemeyer, March 5, 1852).

Thus the Marxist theory of class struggle can only be understood in connection with the basic tenets of historical materialism. This struggle is explained in terms of its historical origins, development, and limits, on the basis of definite and changing economic conditions. This *historical* view was for Marx the decisive element, and Lenin later explained, on the basis of further experience, just what this meant concretely. Lenin pointed out that Kautsky, regarded in his day as the most authoritative writer on Marxist theory, when faced with the First World War and the Russian Revolution of 1917, was unable to go beyond what Marx called the bourgeois limit of recognizing the class struggle, and could not recognize the dictatorship of the proletariat and the transition to socialism. Thus:

> This is the touchstone on which the real understanding and acceptance of Marxism should be tested. And it is not surprising that when the history of Europe brought the working class face to face with this question in a

practical way, not only all the opportunists and reformists, but all the Kautskyists (those who vacillate between reformism and Marxism) proved to be miserable Philistines and petty-bourgeois democrats who repudiated the dictatorship of the proletariat . . . Opportunism does not carry the recognition of class struggle to the main point, to the period of *transition* from capitalism to socialism, to the period of overthrow and complete abolition of the bourgeoisie. *(State and Revolution)*

What is essential here, therefore, is to see that Marx's theory of class and class struggle is not a theory only of the structure and function of society, a way of explaining a given social order, after the manner of orthodox sociology, or even of the classical political economists. It is, on the contrary, that section of Marx's theory which scientifically reflects the process by which 'the whole thing is smashed up'. It is concerned with the creation, consolidation and rendering conscious, of the working class, the force which effects the political changes necessary to abolish the classes made redundant by the development of production and places itself in power.

The classes which Marx writes about are definite, historically necessary organs of an historical mode of production; the politics and ideology of these classes, or of sections of them, are reflections of their historical economic interests, though of course the same warnings must be made for the *form* and *mode* of this reflection as Engels made for the ideological process in general.

Lenin has given what is the most general definition of 'class' in the Marxist sense:

> Classes are large groups of people which differ from each other by the place they occupy in a historically definite system of social production, by their relation (in most cases fixed and formulated in laws) to the means of production, by their role in the social organization of labour, and consequently, by the dimensions and method of acquiring the share of social wealth that they obtain. Classes are groups of people one of which may appropriate the labour of another owing to the different places they occupy in the definite system of social economy. *(Collected Works* 29, p. 421)

There is an unbridgeable gulf between this Marxist view of the objective basis of social class and the notion of class in bourgeois sociology. Schumpeter, for example, expresses clearly what many others accept by implication. Complaining that classes are often assumed to exist on a socio-economic basis, he writes '. . . these classes are classes only in the sense that they result from the scholar's classification of economic subjects'. Dahrendorf has more recently endorsed this essentially idealist standpoint. For him, classes with only latent interests are 'quasi-groups', and exist only as theoretical constructions: 'Only by doubtful analogy can we talk about the "members" of such quasi-groups.' (*Class and Class Conflict in Industrial Society*, p. 179). The mystery deepens when we learn in the next paragraph that 'On the other hand, common modes of behaviour are characteristic of interest groups recruited from larger quasi-groups'. A remarkable type of recruitment, since 'only by doubtful analogy' do these quasi-groups have any members! Schumpeter tells us further that, '... The ultimate foundation on which the class phenomenon rests consists of individual differences in aptitude.' (*Capitalism, Socialism and Democracy*). Though Schumpeter refines this definition by qualifying aptitude as 'socially necessary', he only thereby renders it tautological, as it turns out to be a matter of aptitude for being in the given classes. There is here a stark and obvious contrast with the Marxist insistence on the historical-economic 'ultimate foundations' of classes, to which individual aptitudes conform through the division of labour and all the institutions of the superstructure.

The spate of studies of 'social mobility', particularly those concerned with the working class, show very clearly that bourgeois sociology accepts the class structure as 'given'. It does not go beyond the naive 'realism' of the American sociologist Cooley: '... the relation between the employing and hand-labouring classes is first of all a matter of personal attitudes.' Lipset and Bendix in 1959 were able to conclude similarly: '... the *cumulation* of disadvantages at the bottom of the social scale is in large part the result of a lack of interest [!] in educational and occupational achievements'. (p. 285)

Talcott Parsons, always the most explicit of sociologists in his rejection of the claim for objectivity made by Marxism, proposes instead a starting-point justified on the purest pragmatic grounds. (It can be said in general that behind the mountainous 'theoretical' and abstract constructions of Parsons always stands the crudest pragmatism, in the philosophical sense. One reason why this goes unrecognized is that pragmatism itself is not seen as the basically 'subjective' philosophy which Pierce, James and Dewey made of it, whatever their differences.) Parsons rejects Marxism as a basis for examining the role of ideas in society because its explanations are '... almost uniformly couched in genetic, historical terms, as the Marxist theory itself is, and analytical generalizations as to the role of ideas cannot in principle be proved or disproved by such a method'. In other words,

Parsons will interpret any specific ideas, and their relation to given 'social action', in terms of some supposedly universally valid 'generalizations' about the role of ideas, explicitly abstracting from the specific content and *historical* role of these ideas, their particular origin and development in a given struggle of material forces. That it should be this very historical 'specificness', materially determined, which is the key to the 'role of ideas', is beyond the range of Parsons' conceptual apparatus. (*Essays in Sociological Theory*, p. 26)

The real result of the apparent 'value-neutrality' and refusal of any 'philosophical' assumptions is to embrace an idealism which repeats the assertions of Schumpeter, that reality is essentially a matter of what the observer decides. But Parsons goes further, and transfers these subjective notions into the centre of the social reality under observation. For example, having decided to concentrate on the moral aspect of stratification, Parsons takes up the objection that this procedure might be considered arbitrary:

> It is, however, no more and no less arbitrary than, for instance, the selection of distance as a basic category for describing the relations of bodies in a mechanical system [sic]. Its selection is determined by the place which moral evaluation holds in a generalized conceptual scheme, the 'theory of action'. The only necessary justification of such a selection at the outset is to show that the categories are applicable [?]. In our ordinary treatment of social rank, moral evaluations are in fact prominently involved. The normal reaction to a conspicuous error in ranking is at least in part one of moral indignation — either a person thinks he is 'unjustly' disparaged by being put on a level with those who are really his inferiors, or his real superiors feel 'insulted' by having him, in the relevant aspects, treated as their equal. (*Ibid.*, p. 70)

It is difficult to know where to start, so complete is the conceptual confusion: the words 'applicable', 'ordinary', 'normal', 'conspicuous error', 'really', and 'real superiors' all refer precisely to what needs to be demonstrated, and not at all to some universally agreed reality. To paraphrase Marx's rhetorical question: if the social reality is directly reflected in the consciousness of the actors, what then is the need for social science?

The purpose of this digression is to indicate that the philosophical assumptions of sociology, even where they assert themselves, as in the vast majority of cases, through the mechanism of proceeding without examining in any way what one's assumptions are, affect fundamentally the categories and criteria of selection and significance of what is called 'the empirical data'. We cannot therefore simply compare the findings of Marx with those of other sociologists and ask which 'fit the facts', or whether the one can be 'supplemented' by the other. It is a question of the relation between the category 'class' and the whole theory of interpenetration between society and nature, subject and object, economy and superstructure.

It is this which Lenin insists upon when he comments upon Marx's assertion that besides the class struggle, its origins and its outcome, the implications of acceptance of the theory must be worked out. Sociology's claim to 'value-freedom' is precisely its rejection of these implications.

Yet another dimension of Marxism, as opposed to 'sociology', must be interposed at this stage of the discussion. The working class — and of course the other classes in relationship with it — must be studied from the point of view of what it is *becoming through struggle,* and not simply from the standpoint of defining its role in the existing society. The consciousness by the working class of this role is already an element in the process of abolishing itself as a class, but no less essential is the actual struggle of the working class against the domination of these laws and the political system produced by their operation.

'In the ordinary run of things,' the labourer can be left to the natural laws of production. Direct force, i.e. the coercive force of the state, is used 'only exceptionally', when the proletariat through its struggle resists the dehumanizing effects of these laws of capitalist production in such a way as to threaten capitalist rule. Only social revolution can end the relation of wage-labour sold as a commodity to capital.

But the struggle towards this revolution has resulted at times in reforms, partial victories. A Marxist could not write a 'sociology' of class structure and class conflict without critically analysing these actual efforts of the oppressed classes to become something other than what their oppressors make them. Marx, for example, describes the factory legislation of 19th century Britain as a victory of the political economy of the working class over the political economy of the bourgeoisie. This view was part and parcel of his notion of the working class as a force which would conquer its own emancipation and in the process abolish itself and class society. Lassalle, in glaring contrast, always spoke in terms of the 'iron law' of wages, and appropriately elaborated a programme of 'State socialism' under the benevolent gaze of the dictator Bismarck.

Class and 'size of income'

This emphasis on conflict (struggle) in the Marxist theory of class is part of that historical or dialectical standpoint which distinguishes Marxism from sociology. Where sociology sees concepts like 'class' as terms or concepts which provide more or less useful tools for the description of the functions of a particular society, or as building-blocks for 'models' which elucidate these functional interrelations, Marxism is always seeking the 'law of motion' of a given social order, the mode of development by which it both reproduces its characteristic features and at the same time generates the conditions of its own negation. Marx's aim, therefore, is not to look for a set of categories of class which will suitably classify, with the minimum number of anomalies, the individual members of the society. He is in fact interested in the actions and utterances of these individuals only in so far as they express with particular sharpness the course of development of classes or sections of classes. All theories of class which are designed to 'classify' the population can be excluded from discussion about Marx's theory.

One other common misunderstanding may be cleared away at this preliminary stage by pursuing the latter point. When Marx writes about class struggle he is talking about irreconcilable antagonistic interests rooted in basic relations of production. This clash of interests does not arise from adding together the individual conflicts undergone by individual members of the same class, but from the exploitation relationship and its changes, together with the political steps taken to assure its continuation. All sorts of other conflicts occur in society and are related to class conflict in different ways, but the class conflict is decisive historically, because it is directly related to the development of the mode of production, its conditions of relative stability, its contradictions and its change into its opposite.

By way of example, contrast this Marxist view with another approach to social stratification which is often described as 'objective' in character, viz., classification of the population by size of income (whether this be the sole or only one of several 'objective characteristics' taken into account). In the first place, Marx's theory is strictly speaking not one of 'stratification', but of the process by which the forces of transformation of one form of society into another are necessarily born and develop (and, as a by-product, how the ruling class is able for a considerable period to ensure a relative equilibrium or *modus vivendi* between the contending forces).

Secondly, differences in size of income divide men as individuals from each other just as surely within a given class as across class lines. 'The size of one's purse is a purely quantitative difference, by which any two individuals of the *same class* may be brought into conflict.'

The last point may emerge more clearly if posed in another way: the magnitudes of individual incomes form a series, more or less a continuum, and each income is, without doubt, an 'objective' datum; but the points at which 'class' lines are drawn horizontally across this continuum is an entirely *subjective* matter decided by the analyst; no matter where a line is drawn, it is evident that many individuals on different sides of it will have more in common than each of them has with others included with him in the same 'class'. In other words, despite the 'objective' criterion (size of income) here used, the term 'class' has only the significance of 'classification' according to the requirements of the investigator. (And for such purely subjective purposes, Parsons' insistence that virtually *any* starting-point will do must be accepted.)

Marx, on the other hand, sees classes as the outgrowth of the basic needs of society's production, and seeks a *theory* of class which expresses the actual relation, in development, between the classes. Certainly the classes are related to each other, opposed to each other, in every sphere of social life, including the most remote realms of ideology, and the investigator may choose to select any one of these sets of relations. But the further away he moves from the sphere of production, Marx would argue, the more likely he is to seize upon differences and relationships which are transitory, confined to a given sphere of activity, and even quite ephemeral. A dialectical definition of class must begin from where the antagonistic relations themselves originate, and develop concepts which accurately trace the reflection of this fundamental conflict. In this way Marx's view of class is inseparable from his historical materialist theory of base and superstructure.

For Marx, a 'class' is not an aggregate of all those with similar incomes or even possessions, but consists of all those with a similar property relation *to the means of production*, and thereby to other classes who stand in a different property relation. The sphere of *consumption* is secondary, derived. A scientific concept will indicate the derivation and development, not summarize the end-product.

Sociologists who proceed in the latter manner would qualify for the verdict pronounced on bourgeois economists in Vol. III of *Capital*, in which:

> ... it will be shown what the Philistine's and vulgar economist's way of looking at things stems from, namely from the fact that it is only the direct form of manifestation of relations that is reflected in their brains and not their *inner connection*. Incidentally, if the latter were the case, what would be the need of science? (Marx, letter to Engels, June 27, 1867.)

Very often a definition will be given which appears 'objective', even to the extent of taking into account Marx's view and adding to it other features, yet such definitions are used as classifications rather than as concepts which are part of a whole historical theory of society. Dahrendorf's refutation of Marx's theory of class, for example, proceeds from such a definition: 'Thus we follow Sering in expecting the typical capitalist to be at the same time the legal owner of his factory, the practical manager of production, and the supreme commander of his workers.' The class of capitalists will consequently consist of all these 'typical capitalists'. A highly convenient definition! It then only remains to show that these 'typical' roles have been 'differentiated' in order to prove that the capitalist class 'no longer exists'.

'Source of income' and class

Before Marx, the political economists of the classical school, culminating in Adam Smith and Ricardo, had analysed in detail the distribution of the product between different classes, which manifested itself as a law in and through the apparently chance and accidental play of the market. This definition of classes — according to respective source of income — was the highest point reached within bourgeois social theory on this question. It requires a leap beyond the limits of the historical conditions of capitalist production to penetrate deeper than these distribution relations.

Marx concerned himself, as we have seen, with the basic social relations of production underlying the mode of distribution; relations of production which were themselves historical, i.e. transitory as well as necessary products. Where the political economists took these production relations as natural (and this was true even of Millar and the whole Scottish school, who outlined the economic basis of all 'ranks',) Marx sought their origin and law of development. If the production relations of a society, and the new production relations which would replace them, were themselves historical products, then the classes in which men struggle to reproduce and produce them must be analysed at this level of production first of all.

Once again we find that the outstanding Marxists, such as Lenin, Trotsky and Rosa Luxemburg, have always defended this conception of class against those who proceeded from more simplified and descriptive definitions, which in essence were restricted to the surface of society. Lenin, in one of his many criticisms of the unhistorical and idealistic views of the Narodniks, says:

> To look for the fundamental distinguishing feature of the various classes of society in their sources of income is to give precedence to relations of distribution, which in reality are only a consequence of relations of production. This error was long ago pointed out by Marx, who described as vulgar socialists those who failed to see it. The fundamental criterion by which classes are distinguished is the place they occupy in social production, and, consequently, the relations in which they stand to the means of production. Appropriation of one part or another of the social means of production and its application to private enterprise, to undertakings organized for the sale of the product, is the fundamental distinction of one class in present society (the bourgeoisie) from the proletariat, which is deprived of the means of production and sells its labour power.
>
> . . . it is the exploitation of wage-labour that leads to the division of society into irreconcilably opposed classes, and . . . only from the point of view of this class struggle can all other manifestations of exploitation be consistently gauged.

Engels notes that in Marx's method, 'Every economic relation is first conceived from the point of view of production, apart from all historical determination'. Capitalist society itself facilitates the abstraction of 'economic' from other characteristics of social differentiation, because of the necessary conditions of its own emergence and daily reproduction, i.e. the freeing of wage-labour and capital from all except economic ties.

A common objection to historical materialism is that its notion of economic relations as the 'base' is a reflection of capitalist society's own pre-eminent concern with economic or 'material' considerations, whereas in other forms of society religion or politics predominated in social relations. A German newspaper in America criticized Marx's *Contribution to the Critique of Political Economy* (1859) on precisely these grounds, and Marx replies:

In the estimate of that paper, my view that each special mode of production and the social relations corresponding to it, in short, that the economic structure of society, is the real basis on which the juridical and political superstructure is raised, and to which definite social forms of thought correspond; that the mode of production determines the character of the social, political, and intellectual life generally, all this is very true for our own times, in which material interests preponderate, but not for the middle ages, in which Catholicism, nor for Athens and Rome, where politics, reigned supreme.

In the first place it strikes one as an odd thing for any one to suppose that these well-worn phrases about the middle ages and the ancient world are unknown to anyone else. This much, however, is clear, that the middle ages could not live on Catholicism, nor the ancient world on politics. On the contrary, it is the mode in which they gained a livelihood that explains why here politics, and there Catholicism, played the chief part. For the rest, it requires but a slight acquaintance with the history of the Roman republic, for example, to be aware that its secret history is the history of its landed property. On the other hand, Don Quixote long ago paid the penalty for wrongly assuming that knight errantry was compatible with all economical forms of property.

The feudal 'estates' and differences of rank had to be wiped out in order to allow commodities to confront each other with perfect freedom. 'Equality before the law' was added to 'Equality in the sight of God'. This was especially necessary for the essential commodity, labour-power: in order for it to be bought and sold on the market its possessor, the proletarian, must be free from all oppressive legal ties, able to dispose of his commodity like every other citizen.

Thus far bourgeois social and economic theory. But to expose the historical basis in changing production relations of these economic mechanisms necessitated what Marx called 'the standpoint of socialized humanity' and not 'the standpoint of the isolated individual in civil society'. It was in the production relations that the source of overthrow of bourgeois society was to be found. Only on the basis of these considerations can we understand why Marx's unfinished chapter LII of *Capital*, Vol. III, entitled 'Classes', has been so consistently neglected.

It is in a sense the *coup de grâce* of his whole 'critique of political economy'. Here he returns to the *dissolution* of the 'economic' categories in the real movement which puts an end to the society of which the categories are the reflection. A certain amount of direct quotation is necessary. Marx's intention in Volume III was to explode the solutions hitherto provided by Smith, Ricardo, etc., showing that the contradictions in them were resolved by the recognition of surplus value and its consequences for the division of income and that having thus gone behind the 'apparent movement' to which political economy was restricted, it was possible to proceed to the struggle of classes which actually would settle the fate of the capitalist mode of production.

Marx explained what he was about in a letter to Engels (April 30, 1868):

> At last we have arrived at the *forms of appearance* which serve as the starting point in the vulgar conception: ground rent coming from the earth, profit (interest) from capital, wages from labour. But from our point of view the thing is now seen differently. The apparent movement is explained. Moreover, A. Smith's nonsense, which has become the *main pillar* of all economics hitherto, that the price of a commodity is derived from those three revenues, i.e., only from variable capital (wages) and surplus value (ground rent, profit, interest), is overthrown. The whole movement takes place in this apparent form. Finally since these three (wages, ground rent, profit (interest) constitute the respective sources of income of the three classes of landowners, capitalists and wage labourers, we have, in conclusion, the *class struggle*, into which the movement of the whole *Scheisse* (shit) is resolved.

The last sentence of this quotation may be taken as the starting point of the unfinished chapter 'Classes' (Vol. III of *Capital*). First Marx states that sources of income are rooted in opposed property or non-property in the means of production, and this must be borne in mind for the remainder of the text:

> The owners merely of labour-power, owners of capital, and landowners, whose respective sources of income are wages, profit and ground-rent, in other words, wage-labourers, capitalists and landowners, constitute the three great classes of modern society based upon the capitalist mode of production.

Next, Marx acknowledges that even in England, where 'modern society is indisputably most highly and classically developed in economic structure . . . the stratification of classes does not appear in its pure form'. He does not ignore the existence of intermediate and transitional strata, but simply abstracts from them at this level of analysis: 'Middle and intermediate strata even here obliterate lines of demarcation everywhere (though incomparably less in rural districts than in the cities). However, this is immaterial for our analysis.'

In other contexts, and specifically the political, Marx of course paid great attention to these 'impurities'.

This 'abstraction' is not arbitrary, according to Marx, but itself reflects the process by which capitalism is actually crushing out all non-capitalist forms of production and social groups:

> We have seen that the continual tendency and law of development of the capitalist mode of production is more and more to divorce the means of production from labour, and more and more to concentrate the scattered means of production into large groups, thereby transforming labour into wage-labour and the means of production into capital. And to this tendency, on the other hand, corresponds the independent separation of landed property from capital and labour, or the transformation of all landed property into the form of landed property corresponding to the capitalist mode of production.

Now Marx turns to the general question, 'What constitutes a class?' and says he will proceed to answer it through the answer to another question: 'What makes wage-labourers, capitalists and landlords constitute the three great social classes?' He first of all proceeds to show why source of income, which *appears* to be the answer, is inadequate; '*At first glance* — the identity of revenues and sources of revenue . . .' (my emphasis — C.S.) This 'appearance' is then presented in its everyday form:

> There are three great social groups whose members, the individuals forming them, live on wages, profit and ground rent respectively, on the realization of their labour-power, their capital, and their landed property.

However, says Marx, there are many other, smaller divisions which would more exactly classify the population according to source of income. All these social groups are not, however, social classes like the 'three great social classes'. Thus:

> However, from this standpoint, physicians and officials, e.g., would also constitute two classes, for they belong to two distinct social groups, the members of each of these groups receiving their revenue from one and the same source. The same would also be true of the infinite fragmentation of interest and rank into which the division of social labour splits labourers as well as capitalists and landlords — the latter, e.g., into owners of vineyards, farm owners, owners of forests, mine owners and owners of fisheries . . .(*Ibid*., p. 863)

At this point the manuscript breaks off. We have indicated earlier that Marx's exposition would have been an expansion of the first sentence of his chapter, where types of ownership and non-ownership in means of production, giving rise to a definite, historically-conditioned form of exploitation, are placed at the root of the three main types of source of income and class under capitalism.

This is confirmed not only by the general character of Marx's writings, but particularly by the preceding chapters in Volume III and the various letters he wrote to Engels on his purpose in section VII of this volume. These earlier chapters are devoted specifically to dispelling the illusion that the three types of revenue (wages, profit and ground-rent) are 'realizations' of labour-power, capital and landed property. These three types of ownership are the bases of the three great classes, but it is not true that their respective types of income are rewards or 'realizations' of their respective contributions to production. Much of Volume III is taken up with a detailed disproof of such notions and an exposition of how these characteristic ideological illusions arise. It is shown that, in fact, labour is the source of all these incomes: first of wages; but also of ground-rent and of the profits of the various types of capitalist, which are each proportions of the total surplus-value, the unpaid labour of the proletariat.

Capitalists, landed proprietors and workers

Marx first attacks the absence of any coherence in the usual 'Trinity Formula' (capital-profit, land-rent, labour-wages): '. . . the alleged sources of the annually available wealth belong to widely dissimilar spheres and are not at all analogous with one another. They have about the same relation to each other as lawyer's fees, red beets and music.' Capital is 'a definite social production relation', belonging to a definite historical formation of society; land is 'inorganic nature as such'; and labour as such is an abstraction from all the actual productive types of labour. The latter two are evidently prerequisites of production in any and every mode of production, whereas the first is a definite, historically limited social relation of a certain mode of production. As an explanation of the division of total value (a homogeneous substance) in the society, the 'Trinity Formula' is therefore absurd.

In so far as land contributes to production it does so as *use value*. There is no way whatsoever of measuring this against the *value* represented in capital's share of the total product: '. . . how should land create value, i.e. a socially defined quantity of labour, and moreover that particular portion of the value of its own products which forms the rent?' (*Capital*, Volume III, pp. 794 and 796)

Capital itself is, of course, one historically developed and determined form of an essential prerequisite of all production, viz, the accumulated means of production available to society: but in this case these means of production enter the productive process only when transformed into capital.

The reality, says Marx, is that value, the creation of social labour, is the source of the incomes of all the three great classes. The *proletariat's* sale of labour-power entitles it to *that portion of the total value which is necessary for its own reproduction,* i.e., to replace the value of the labour-power; its share is not based on its contribution to the product (since it is responsible for the total value added to the product), but only on the value of labour-power. The *capitalists,* through ownership of means of production, extract from the whole social labour the entire remaining surplus product as *surplus value.* But this extraction reaches its 'limit' at the point where the *landlord* is in a position to demand a *share* of the total surplus value.

This share arises not from the 'contribution' of his land to the product (which *as value* does not exist), but from the specific relation of land ownership to the capitalist mode of production and the bourgeois class: his ownership of land enables him to put pressure on the capitalist, to extort a share of the surplus; his concentrated landholdings are themselves fixed historically at the outset of the capitalist system as the means by which wage-labour was freed from the land for capitalist exploitation; and in the functioning of capitalist production he 'appears as the personification of one of the most essential conditions of production'. (*Ibid.*, pp. 800-801.)

What is essential here is the historical unity of these class relations in a given mode of production, and their shares in the homogeneous substance of value as the proof of the real interdependence and exploitative, conflicting relations between them. The 'matter of fact' theory which would see them as simple 'contributions' to the ongoing 'industrial society' is completely lacking in any such consistency or unity. 'Conflict', 'tension', etc. are added as afterthoughts or as formulae to cover awkward examples of 'temporary disturbances of equilibrium' instead of being demonstrated as central to the whole system, giving it a specific historical character as a particular mode of production and also providing the key to its transformation into another. This transformation is thus, in Marxism, literally removed from the sphere of prescriptions for 'improving industrial relations', or 'reducing the effects of alienation', etc. as it so often appears in the work of sociological 'critics' of 'industrial society' (see especially the work of Georges Friedmann).

For Marx, then, the total value produced by social labour, through the property relations of the capitalist system, is converted into three different sources of revenue. These sources are real, objective in character, but they do not and cannot explain what creates the real source of all three incomes, namely 'value-creating labour'. Once this source is recognized, then the shares of capital and landed property can be seen as the result of exploitation made possible by property ownership in a definite, historically limited social system.

If, on the contrary, the three 'sources of income' are considered *sufficient* for the definition of what constitutes the basis of the given classes, then these classes appear to result from naturally necessary roles in 'industrial production'. Instead of a revolutionary critique, we have a veritable apologia, an ideology going under the name of economics or sociology:

> It is therefore just as natural that vulgar economy, which is no more than a didactic, more or less dogmatic, translation of everyday conceptions of the actual agents of production, and which arranges them in a certain rational order, should see precisely in this trinity (capital-interest [profit], land-ground rent, labour-wages) which is devoid of all inner connection, the natural and indubitable lofty basis for its shallow pompousness. (*Ibid*, p.810.)

We leave for a later chapter Marx's development of this theme, in which he shows, with very intricate analysis, how the illusions about revenues are reinforced by the essential nature of the capitalist system itself (see *Capital*, Vol. III, Chapter XLVIII 'The Trinity Formula').

Our main purpose has been only to show that Marx's theory of class, in the one social system — capitalism — for which it was worked out, cannot be deduced from the immediately perceptible relations in social life, but on the contrary must penetrate beneath them to the specific production relations, 'the specific economic form, in which unpaid social labour is pumped out of the direct producers' (p. 772). In feudal society, landed property entitled its holders to the unpaid surplus labour of the direct producers, but the 'specific economic form' in which this was done was, of course, entirely different from that whereby landed property shares in the total surplus value pumped out of the working class by capital in capitalist society. In feudal society, a portion of this surplus value was appropriated directly and nakedly in the form of a definite number of days per week or per year spent on the land of the landowner instead of on the land allotted to the serf. Besides this 'labour rent' the landlord would have the right to a definite amount of rent in kind, a proportion of the harvest from the serf's own land (often 'commuted' into cash payments). The exploitation-relation is open, transparent, as contrasted with the apparently free sale of labour power at its value under capitalism.

The theoretical clarification of the distinction between the commodity labour power, bought at its value, and the value created when it is consumed as labour, was a vital stage in the development of Marxist theory, as it turned to the practice of the working class struggle, transcending the previous conceptions of bourgeois political economy and sociology.

Marx's treatment of ground-rent is a good illustration of his analytical-historical method. Landed property, its role in modern capitalist economy, its place in the class struggle, etc., must be viewed *not* as an extension or development of 'landed property' at an earlier (i.e. feudal) stage of social development, but in specific relation to the mode of production within which it now exists, and in relation to the latter's history. For example, the way in which the old type of landed property and the title it gave to the produce of labour was *transformed*, and the small proprietors resulting from its break-up were expropriated, is of more importance in this context than the history of that period in which landed property was the dominant form of property in the means of production. The analysis of ground-rent (and the same would go for money, merchant capital, and other categories) in Vol. III of *Capital* therefore is an expansion of the methodological indications to be found in concentrated form in the posthumously published 'Introduction' to Marx's *Contribution to the Critique of Political Economy:*

> Capital is the all-dominating power of bourgeois society. It must form the starting-point as well as the end and be developed [i.e., in the presentation of the analysis of capitalism —C.S.] before land-ownership is... It would therefore be impractical and wrong to arrange the economic categories in the order in which they were the determining factors in the course of history. The order of sequence is rather determined by the relation which they bear to one another in modern bourgeois society, and which is the exact opposite of what seems to be their natural order or their historical

development. What we are interested in is not the place which economic relations occupy in the historical succession of different forms of society ... we are interested in their organic connection with modern bourgeois society. (Chicago 1904, pp. 808-14)

This outline of Marx's theory of the economic basis of classes brings out the essential unity of his historical materialist outlook in one other way, which must be mentioned if only in answer to some of Marx's critics.

In Chapter II, above, Engels' letters of the 1890s on historical materialism were quoted. It was indicated that these letters, stressing the interaction of base and superstructure, and the relative autonomy of superstructural elements in elaborating social and cultural forms, were in no way just an afterthought to account for unforeseen difficulties in the application of the original theory. The following quotation from Vol. III of *Capital* is given as an example of Marx's own acceptance of this viewpoint.

The specific role played by law in relation to production, the different significance of custom and tradition in specific historical formations, and, most brilliant of all, portrayal of the way in which a custom necessarily enshrined in law to provide the feudal system with stability actually opens the way for new social relations and higher productivity to mature over a long period underneath it, thus turning it into its opposite, are here shown in outline as part of the general preparation of the transition from feudalism to capitalism:

> Since the direct producer (in feudal society) is not the owner, but only a possessor, and since all his surplus labour *de jure* actually belongs to the landlord, some historians have expressed astonishment that it should be at all possible for those subject to enforced labour, or serfs, to acquire any independent property, or relatively speaking, wealth, under such circumstances. However, it is evident that tradition must play a dominant role in the primitive and undeveloped circumstances on which these social production relations and the corresponding mode of production are based. It is furthermore clear that here as always it is in the interest of the ruling section of society to sanction the existing order as law and to legally establish its limits given through usage and tradition. Apart from all else, this, by the way, comes about of itself as soon as the constant reproduction of the basis of the existing order and its fundamental relations assumes a regulated and orderly form in the course of time. And such regulation and order are themselves indispensable elements of any mode of production, if it is to assume social stability and interdependence from mere chance and arbitrariness. These are precisely the form of its social stability and there-

fore its relative freedom from mere arbitrariness and mere chance. Under backward conditions of the production process as well as the corresponding social relations, it achieves this form by mere repetition of their very reproduction. If this has continued on for some time, it entrenches itself as custom and tradition and is finally sanctioned as an explicit law.

However, since the form of this surplus-labour, enforced labour, is based upon the imperfect development of all social productive powers and the crudeness of the methods of labour itself, it will naturally absorb a relatively much smaller portion of the direct producer's total labour than under-developed modes of production, particularly the capitalist mode of production. Take it, for instance, that the enforced labour for the landlord originally amounted to two days per week. These two days of enforced labour per week are thereby fixed, are a constant magnitude, legally regulated by prescriptive or written law. But the productivity of the remaining days of the week, which are at the disposal of the direct producer himself, is a variable magnitude, which must develop in the course of his experience, just as the new wants he acquires, and just as the expansion of the market for his product and the increasing assurance with which he disposes of this portion of his labour-power will spur him on to a greater exertion of his labour-power, whereby it should not be forgotten that the employment of his labour-power is by no means confined to agriculture, but includes rural home industry. The possibility is here presented for definite economic development taking place, of course, upon favourable circumstances, inborn racial characteristics, etc. (*Capital*, Volume III, pp. 773-774.)

An example: the class nature of the USSR

The above remarks are only the ABC of the Marxist theory of class, and the only justification for repeating this ABC is that it is almost universally misunderstood, because both adherents and opponents of Marxism have preferred second-hand accounts of the basic questions and neglected Marx's own work on the economic relations. An acquaintance with the political writings of Marx, Engels and others is certainly necessary, but will not have its real value except on this basis of economic analysis, which gives the political and ideological aspects their historical perspective. In other words, we have so far expanded only on the first point made by Marx in his letter to Weydemeyer, that each type of class struggle is bound up with a certain historical formation of society, derived from the development of the mode of production.

All of Marx's and Engels' writings on the revolutions of 1848, for example, so often quoted for their analysis of the political forces at work, take their meaning from the historical turning-point marked by the French events of that year: the dawn of the proletarian revolutionary struggle against capitalism, rising in such a way as to cripple and distort any possibility of the completion of the bourgeois revolution in continental Europe, by the bourgeoisie itself.

Even though capitalism proved to have before it a longer span than Marx and Engels then anticipated, it is the historical background of this juncture of two epochs, which provides the content of the political and ideological tendencies analysed in the writings on 1848. In similar fashion, Lenin's polemics against the Russian Narodniks in the 1890s, from which we have quoted, revolved around the same axis. The problem of problems was not to find on the surface a potentially 'revolutionary' class in Russian society, but first of all to expose the forms of production which were developing to the exclusion of old forms, and thereby destroying the foundations of old classes.

Once this was done, the historical tasks before the existing classes, their interrelations, the limits of their political action and programmes, and the ideologies and theories appropriate to them, had to be analysed; and these are in fact the problems dealt with in the hundreds of articles, pamphlets and books written by Lenin in that period. Similarly Trotsky, introducing Harold Isaacs' book *The Tragedy of the Chinese Revolution* explains the author's method as an inquiry into the following questions:

> What are the classes which are struggling in China? What are the interrelationships of these classes? How, and in what direction, are these relations being transformed? What are the objective tasks of the Chinese Revolution, i.e., those tasks dictated by the course of development? On the shoulders of which classes rests the solution of these tasks? With what method can they be solved?

These methodological pointers indicate the main lines of approach to a question which must, of course, be a primary one for contemporary Marxism: the class nature of the USSR.

This is not the place to survey the apparently interminable discussion in bourgeois sociology about 'convergence' of Soviet and western capitalist societies, or the associated controversies around the term 'industrial society', resurrected from Comte and Saint-Simon. We are immediately concerned with Marxist theory itself, though of course a more thorough exposition of any aspect of it would necessitate an analysis of all alternative and opposed theories. In any case, however, it will be found that the basic development of sociology on these questions proceeds from a clash with Marxism, in the writings of Max Weber, Durkheim, Pareto, Michels, etc., or from revisions of Marxism originating inside the Marxist movement. Wittfogel's *Oriental Despotism*, for example, was the product of a long evolution on Wittfogel's own part from his early membership of the Communist movement in Germany, and then in the Soviet Union to his present anti-communist standpoint.

Another influential work, James Burnham's *The Managerial Revolution*, has recently been the subject of academic detective work, from which it transpires that Burnham, in the late 1930s a member of the Socialist Workers' Party in the USA (followers of Trotsky), was deeply indebted, to use parliamentary language, to the little-known work of one Bruno Rizzi (Bruno R. *La Bureaucratization du Monde* Paris 1939). A few months before *The Managerial Revolution* was written, Burnham engaged in a bitter controversy with Trotsky on the nature of the USSR and the tasks posed to socialists by the Hitler-Stalin pact, a controversy in which Trotsky drew attention to the work of 'Bruno R'. While the most detailed exposition of Trotsky's views on the social nature of the Soviet Union is his *The Revolution Betrayed*, it was in this polemic with Burnham and Shachtman in the Socialist Workers' Party that his method on the question was made most explicit. It contrasts sharply not only with Burnham's book, with its crude and shallow comparisons and unsupported generalizations, but also with the plethora of terminological experiments which pass for 'theory' inside and outside the socialist movement on this problem.

Trotsky follows closely the method outlined by Marx, insisting first and foremost on historical perspective. Where must the analysis begin, for a Marxist? Not from comparisons of the privileges and wealth or forms of political power characterizing the bureaucrats of the USSR and the capitalists of the West or the fascist rulers of Germany and Italy, but quite differently:

> Scientifically and politically — and not purely terminologically — the question poses itself as follows: Does the bureaucracy represent a temporary growth on a social organism or has this growth already been transformed into a historically indispensable organ? Social excrescences can be the product of an 'accidental' (i.e. temporary and extraordinary) enmeshing of historical circumstances. A social organ (and such is every class,

including an exploiting class) can take shape only as a result of the deeply-rooted inner needs of production itself. If we do not answer this question, then the entire controversy will degenerate into sterile toying with words. (*In Defence of Marxism*, p.7)

Trotsky then develops the theme that the bureaucracy in the USSR has always been a brake on the technique, culture and economy of the workers' state, whereas, '. . . The historical justification for every ruling class consisted in this — that the system of exploitation it headed raised the development of the productive forces to a new level.'

Trotsky always characterized the Soviet bureaucracy, therefore, as a parasitic growth on the workers' state and the nationalized property of the Soviet Union. His basic reason for doing this was his adherence to Marx's historical materialism in rejecting all sociological analysis based on the external characteristics of social groups and forms of domination. He pointed out to impatient 'left' critics of the Soviet Union that their 'anti-bureaucracy' enthusiasm in characterizing Stalin and his bureaucracy as a new exploiting class was, from the standpoint of Marxism, actually to allot to them a vital and necessary historical role:

> If the Bonapartist riff-raff is a class this means that it is not an abortion but a viable child of history. If its marauding parasitism is 'exploitation' in the scientific sense of the term, this means that the bureaucracy possesses a historical future as the ruling class indispensable to a given system of economy. (*Ibid.*, p.29)

According to Marx, the prerequisites for socialism are developed inside the capitalist mode of production: advanced productive forces in science and industry; international division of labour and world market. The contradiction between these forces of production and capitalist production relations, political, state and ideological forms, prepares the conditions for the social revolution. World capitalism broke first, not at its great advanced centres, but 'at its weakest link' in Russia.

The proletarian revolution is by its nature an international revolution. But yet there is not and cannot be a simultaneous overthrow of capitalism in every country. The conditions for political overthrow of the bourgeoisie in Russia matured in 1917, but were not accompanied in that country by the parallel development of the economic conditions and consequent cultural development necessary for the building of socialism. These conditions were prepared on a world scale.

So long as the revolutionary outpost could be maintained in isolation in Russia, bureaucratic distortions would necessarily appear, because the proletarian dictatorship, containing within itself the beginnings of its own self-destruction by drawing ever wider masses into its work, requires a cultural development which rapidly transforms the whole condition of life of the masses. The isolation of the young Soviet state from the world's advanced centres blocked such a development.

The bureaucracy which arose in these conditions was therefore considered by Trotsky, from the Marxist standpoint, not as the ruling class of some new form of society, but as the result of the temporary isolation of the world revolution in a backward country, a social force extruded from the working class, but which then stands in relation to this same class as a sort of prism to refract all the pressure of the capitalist states remaining outside the USSR and all the survivals of backwardness within. This effect was strengthened decisively for a whole epoch by the series of defeats for the working classes of Italy (1922-1924), Germany (1923,1933), Britain and China (1926-1927), Poland (1926), and Spain (1936-1938). The ideological means by which this bureaucracy established its position (the theory of 'socialism in one country', etc.) relied heavily on the claim for a 'realistic' assessment of these defeats. Here again the interaction between consciousness and economic base is essential to understanding the actual course of events. These very defeats were more and more the consequence of the very policy which received its first impetus from adaptation to the first of these defeats. Here again Trotsky insists on a dialectical analysis as against the matter-of-fact acceptance of the 'relation of class forces' to be found in the 'official' school of Communist Party Marxists and their apologists.

At the same time Trotsky is insisting on the full historical meaning of the term 'class', a meaning which he refuses to 'bureaucracy'. Thus he wrote:

> The class has an exceptionally important and moreover a scientifically restricted meaning to a Marxist. A class is defined not by its participation in the distribution of the national income alone, but by its independent role in the general structure of economy and by its independent roots in the economic foundation of society. Each class (the feudal nobility, the peasantry, the petty bourgeoisie, the capitalist bourgeoisie, and the proletariat) works out its own special forms of property.
>
> The bureaucracy lacks all these social traits. It has no independent position

in the process of production and distribution. It has no independent property roots. Its functions relate basically to the political technique of class rule. The existence of a bureaucracy, in all its variety of forms and differences in specific weight, characterizes every class regime. Its power is of a reflected character. The bureaucracy is indissolubly bound up with a ruling economic class, feeding itself upon the social roots of the latter, maintaining itself and falling together with it. (*The Class Nature of the Soviet State*)

We have deliberately expounded the basic economic arguments of *Capital* Vol. III and Trotsky's analysis of the USSR, first to show the consistency and continuity in the fundamental definition, and secondly, because these two bring out many questions of wide-ranging historical perspectives which would normally not enter the sociological discussion of 'class'.

Marx and Marxists are asking totally different questions from those asked by sociologists when they discuss 'class', or indeed any other social phenomena. The second great difficulty for sociologists in this kind of question is that Marxists write as protagonists of a theory which sees itself as part of the reality it is accounting for, and, more than that, as the conscious expression of the struggle of the working class to grasp and change that reality in its developing totality. The relation between Marxism, class and class consciousness is therefore entirely different from the avowed (and the actual) relation between sociology and society. Our extract from the discussion of the nature of the USSR illustrates this. To understand it further we must now go beyond the 'ABC'. Classes manifest themselves *politically*, in struggle. They have representatives and leaders as well as relatively unconscious layers. They are internally differentiated. Between them and straddling them are transitional and intermediate layers. All these relationships are undergoing constant change. One class, the bourgeoisie, builds up its revolutionary potential under feudalism economically and culturally, 'unconsciously' in a certain sense, while another, the proletariat , is united by its *lack* of any specific 'mode of appropriation' either economically or culturally under capitalism.

The proletariat therefore requires a qualitative leap in consciousness, concentrated towards the taking of political power, which it must then use for the economic transformation of society.

V
Classes and class struggle: politics and revolution

'Class in itself' and 'class for itself'

The struggle of the working class against the bourgeoisie arises from the latter's appropriation of the surplus product of the worker's labour over and above that portion of the product required to replace the value of labour-power purchased in order to set production in motion. In so far as all workers share this characteristic of being exploited because of their ownership only of labour power, which is sold as a commodity, they form a class — a class 'in itself', as Marx, following the expression of Hegel, termed it: but not yet a class 'for itself'. For the latter, a process of development was necessary:

> The political movement of the working class has as its object, of course, the conquest of power for the working class, and for this it is naturally necessary that a previous organization of the working class, itself arising from their economic struggle, should have been developed up to a certain point.
> On the other hand, however, every movement in which the working class comes out as a class against the ruling classes and attempts to force them by pressure from without is a political movement.
> For instance, the attempt in a particular factory or even a particular industry to force a shorter working day out of the capitalists by strikes, etc., is a purely economic movement.
> On the other hand, the movement to force an eight-hour day, etc., by law is a political movement. And in this way, out of the separate economic movements of the workers, there grows up everywhere a political movement, that is to say a movement of the class, with the object of achieving its interests in a general form, in a form possessing a general social force of compulsion ...(Marx, letter to Bolte, November 23, 1871)

Marx is here expanding the concepts put forward in his early works (particularly *The Poverty of Philosophy*, *The Communist Manifesto*): in so far as the proletariat is created by the advance of the bourgeoisie, by its 'other', it constitutes a class 'in itself', 'in relation to capital'. But this is only the precondition for a process: '... in the struggle ...this mass unites and forms itself into a class for itself.'

There is not some metaphysical, predetermined necessity that each class 'in itself' will become a class 'for itself'. It is only in so far as the material struggles forced upon the class make it possible for it to unite and realize itself in political action that this transformation takes place, a transformation which can then bring from the political level of the class's activity a decisive reaction upon the economic level from which it sprang.

As Marx's letter to Weydemeyer (quoted at the beginning of the previous chapter) put it, the class struggle under capitalism leads to the dictatorship of the proletariat and through this to the abolition of classes. The same point is brought out, this time 'negatively', but with a more detailed exposition of its meaning, in Marx's analysis of the peasantry in France in the revolutionary period 1848-1850:

> The small peasants form a vast mass, the members of which live in similar conditions, but without entering into manifold relations with one another. Their mode of production isolates them from one another, instead of bringing them into mutual intercourse.
>
> The isolation is increased by France's bad means of communication and by the poverty of the peasants. Their field of production, the small-holding, admits of no division of labour in its cultivation, no application of science and, therefore, no multiplicity of development, no diversity of talents, no wealth of social relationships.
>
> Each individual peasant family is almost self-sufficient; it itself directly produces the major part of its consumption and thus acquires its means of life more through exchange with nature than in intercourse. with society. The small holding, the peasant and his family; alongside them another small-holding, another peasant and another family. A few score of these make up a village, and a few score of villages make up a Department.
>
> In this way, the great mass of the French nation is formed by simple addition of homologous magnitudes, much as potatoes in a sack form a sackful of potatoes. In so far as millions of families live under economic conditions of existence that divide their mode of life, their interests and their culture from those of the other classes, and put them in hostile contrast to the latter, they form a class.
>
> In so far as there is merely a local interconnection among these small peasants, and the identity of their interests begets no unity, no national union and no political organization, they do not form a class. (*The 18th Brumaire of Louis Bonaparte*, in Selected Works, Volume II, pp. 414-415)

Whereas the proletariat's economic origin constantly leads it into a common struggle, binds it into closer internal relations, forces it to undergo radicalizing experiences in industry through the development of the productive forces (science, communications, technique), and the clash of these forces with the capitalist production relations, and thrusts it towards the necessity of its independent political expression of this common experience as a class, in 'a form possessing a general social force of compulsion', the opposite is true for the small peasants.

The inexorable 'revolutionization of the conditions of production' in the bourgeois epoch certainly affects the peasantry, but, in contrast to the proletariat, in such a way as to dissolve or at least to divide it as a class: some become bigger farmers, but others go down into the proletariat; or, characteristically, peasant agriculture declines and stagnates at the side of big industry and large capitalist farming for whole historical periods, and the members of this class eke out their living and protect their 'independence' in sharper and sharper opposition to the other members of their own class. From time to time they organize collective struggles and protests, which even on the largest scale issue in defeat and despair so long as they are not combined with the development of the proletarian revolution. What then is the characteristic political reflection of the class nature of the small peasantry? Marx answers:

> They are consequently incapable of enforcing their own class interest in their own name, whether through parliament or through a convention. They cannot represent themselves, they must be represented. Their representative must at the same time appear as their master, as an authority over them, as an unlimited governmental power that protects them against the other classes and sends them the rain and the sunshine from above.
> The political influence of the small peasants, therefore, finds its final expression in the executive power subordinating society to itself.

And this small peasantry is the explanation of the latest and highest phase of the development of an executive power of state standing above the classes in France. Thus:

> And yet the state power is not suspended in mid-air. Bonaparte represents a class, and the most numerous class of French society at that, the small peasants.

The potential in the working class of political independence, of its social force achieving an expression which is not simply an affirmation of its oppressed position, which is not used simply to develop quantitatively the existing tendencies in the political life of capitalist society, but can bring about a qualitative, revolutionary transformation, is the essence of the problem around which the development of Marxism in this century has centred, that of working-class consciousness and revolutionary leadership.

What immediately suggests itself is that the working class will require a consciousness which cannot be derived directly or completely from its oppressed position, but which embraces the overall development of society. It is interesting to note Marx's original formulation of this aspect of the problem, in which he describes the proletariat as '. . . . a sphere which does not stand in a one-sided contradiction to the consequences, but in a general and all-round contradiction to the very hypotheses of the German state.' (*Critique of Hegel's Philosophy of Right*, 1843)

In understanding the Marxist view of this problem, it is important to approach it as a process of struggle for working-class consciousness and not in terms of whether a given set of ideas 'fits' the abstractly conceptualized position of the proletariat in society 'in general'. Marxists must obviously answer the question of how to characterize the level of consciousness represented by political leaders of the working class who certainly represent or control organizations at the level of the mobilization of the class as a class, and yet reject the revolutionary outlook of Marxism. It is, of course, not uncommon to find commentators who explain such political ideas by saying that they reflect the class itself and are in this way historically justified. Such an interpretation has nothing to do with Marxism. A political leadership is never the automatic 'reflection' of the economic needs of the class. Political parties and tendencies are formed at the level of the political superstructure, and 'men of politics' take their stamp from the prevailing forces in that sphere so long as they are not engaged in constant and conscious struggle against it with an explicitly critical and revolutionary theory and practice.

> Only vulgar 'Marxists' who take it that politics is a mere and direct 'reflection' of economics, are capable of thinking that leadership reflects the class directly and simply. In reality leadership, having risen above the oppressed class, inevitably succumbs to the pressure of the ruling class. The leadership of the American trade unions, for instance, 'reflects' not so much the proletariat, as the bourgeoisie. (Trotsky, *In Defence of Marxism*, p.14)

Implicit in Trotsky's remarks is the basic point which he himself had so strongly emphasized in his *Literature and Revolution:* the notion of 'economic base-ideological superstructure' is applicable only at the level of society or socio-economic formation. To reduce it to the scale of a particular class, as if the latter had its 'own' base and superstructure is to mutilate the theory. While the conditions of life and experience common to a particular class give a distinctive character to the habits and opinions of its members, it must be borne in mind that the ideological superstructure of the whole society, developed as a reflection and at the same time an instrument of the domination of the ruling class, is concentrated into every ideological and political manifestation in the society, including the spontaneous reactions of the oppressed classes.

If this were not the case, revolution would be an automatic growth, whereas it is in fact the product of, on the one hand, objective economic contradictions, and, on the other, the resolution of an ideological and political crisis in the midst of the revolutionary class itself, in which the old ideological forms are thrown aside and the objective character of the contradictions is perceived.

Class struggle and revolution: the example of 1848

In the revolutions of 1848, Marx and Engels took the opportunity of testing their new theories against historical experience. They had claimed to be 'scientific socialists', basing their political programme on the revolutionary struggle of a class inevitably produced by capitalism's own development. (*The Communist Manifesto*). This they had contrasted with the 'Utopian socialism' of all varieties. 1848 was to bring the industrial proletariat directly on to the political scene, its force actually bringing about great changes in the state. But the result could only be, at this stage, the bourgeois republic. King Louis Philippe, overthrown in February 1848, had presided over the rule of only one section of the bourgeoisie, the 'finance oligarchy'. It still remained for the *industrial* bourgeoisie to 'normalize' the relations between the whole bourgeois class and the state machine. Louis Philippe was overthrown in February 1848 by an alliance of industrial bourgeoisie, proletariat, urban middle class, and peasantry. The Provisional Government then set up could only be a compromise between all the classes which had contributed to the overthrow of Louis Philippe:

> The great majority of its members consisted of representatives of the bourgeoisie. The republican petty bourgeoisie were represented by Ledru-Rollin and Flocon, the republican bourgeoisie by the people from the 'National' (the newspaper of the republican opposition, founded by Thiers in 1830), the dynastic opposition by Crémieux, Dupont de l'Eure, etc.
>
> The working class had only two representatives, Louis Blanc and Albert. Finally, Lamartine as a member of the Provisional Government; the latter had actually no real interest, no definite class, it was the February Revolution itself, the common uprising with its illusions, its poetry, its imagined content and its phrases. For the rest, the spokesman of the February Revolution, by his position and his views belonged to the bourgeoisie. (Marx, *The Class Struggles in France, 1848-1850* in Selected Works, Volume II, p.199)

Marx's analysis of the 1848-1850 events in France is the history of the dramatic dissolution of this political unity under the impact of the irreconcilable class antagonisms between its several components. However, Marx was compelled to explain, by his own theory and method, not only the long-term necessity which eventually prevailed, but also the movement of events, men and ideas which at first sight, by their complexity and accidental character, contradict the materialist conception. How did the compromise arise in the first place? Why did the historical necessity establish itself only through a definite series of stages and struggles? Why were these struggles veiled in particular types of political illusions and not others? And finally, why did the democratic republic brought forth by February 1848, once the working class was defeated and brought into line, quickly submit to the dictatorship of Louis Bonaparte, borne aloft on the shoulders of the humble peasant?

The main criticism levelled against historical materialism is that precisely such questions are left unanswered by the stress on the 'ultimate' determining character of the economic base. The writings of Lenin and Trotsky on the Russian Revolution and the class struggle in this century are certainly the most complete answer. However, Marx and Engels' own writings on 1848 were already sufficient to put paid to this criticism of historical materialism. What follows here is only a series of examples, meant as an introduction to the study of the texts themselves.

Modern 'political sociology' can, of course, afford to neglect the kind of questions dealt with by Marx in 1848-1851. It takes the groups and classes in society simply as accumulations of certain external characteristics (level of education, literacy, income, occupation, area of residence, occupation of parents, etc. etc.) and then checks against these a more or less impressive series of data about what is called 'political behaviour', normally consisting of votes cast in elections. If 'vulgar political economy' was an apologia for capitalist exploitation, political sociology would perhaps have been characterized by Marx as a sort of market research operation for established political parties. Whereas bourgeois 'political sociology' devotes itself entirely to the surface 'political behaviour' of the individuals in society during periods of relative stability, Marx's theory was, characteristically, tested against revolutionary upheavals. His sociology of class cannot be separated from his 'sociology of revolution'.

How does Marx explain the combination of opposed class forces in the Provisional government in 1848? He begins with a characterization of Louis Philippe's regime and the opposition to it:

> It was not the French *bourgeoisie* that ruled under Louis Philippe, but a fraction of it, bankers, stock-exchange kings, railway kings, owners of coal and iron works and forests, a part of the landed proprietors that rallied round them — the so-called *finance aristocracy*. It sat on the throne, it dictated laws in the Chambers, it conferred political posts from cabinet portfolios to the tobacco bureau. (*Ibid.*, p. 193)

The rule of this finance aristocracy produced characteristic political and social contradictions, particularly through its plunder of government finances and control of government agencies. These accumulated in such a way as to render the finance aristocracy the common object and symbol against which all opposition to existing conditions was concentrated. The industrial bourgeoisie formed the core of the parliamentary opposition, and gradually gained in confidence to oppose the regime through the 1840s, comforted by the feeling that the proletariat had been thoroughly disciplined by the suppression of the uprisings of 1832, 1834 (Lyons) and 1839. The other classes which were to appear in the revolutionary struggles of 1848, the petty bourgeoisie and the peasantry, had, like the proletariat, no place whatsoever in the political life of the July monarchy.

Marx summarizes the swindling and extortion of the finance aristocracy through the national debt and the financing of state enterprises, and concludes:

> The July monarchy was nothing other than a joint stock company for the exploitation of French national wealth, the dividends of which were divided among ministers, Chambers, 240,000 voters and their adherents. Louis Philippe was the director of this company — Robert Macaire on the throne. Trade, industry, agriculture, shipping, the interests of the industrial bourgeoisie, were bound to be continually prejudiced and endangered under this system. (*Ibid.*, p. 193)

The moral and cultural decay engendered by this 'official' regime of plunder had its own special part in the production of the revolutionary opposition:

> ... the same prostitution, the same shameless cheating, the same mania to get rich was repeated in every sphere, from the court to the Café Borgne (the term applied to all cafés of dubious reputation), to get rich not by production, but by pocketing the already available wealth of others. In particular there broke out, at the top of bourgeois society, clashing every moment with the bourgeois laws themselves, an unbridled display of unhealthy and dissolute appetites, wherein the wealth having its source in gambling naturally seeks its satisfaction, where pleasure becomes *crapuleux* (debauched), where gold, filth and blood flow together. The finance aristocracy, in its mode of acquisition as well as in its pleasures, is nothing but the resurrection of the lumpenproletariat at the top of bourgeois society. And the non-ruling sections of the French bourgeoisie cried: corruption! The people cried: *a bas les grands voleurs! a bas les assassins!* (Down with the big robbers! Down with the murderers!) when in 1847, on the most prominent stages of bourgeois society, the same scenes were publicly enacted which regularly lead the lumpenproletariat to brothels, to workhouses and lunatic asylums, before the Bench, to Bagnos (a prison) and to the scaffold. The industrial bourgeoisie saw its interests endangered, the petty bourgeoisie was filled with moral indignation, the imagination of the people was offended, Paris was flooded with pamphlets — '*la dynastie Rothschild*', '*les juifs rois de l'époque*' ('The Rothschild dynasty', 'The Jews, kings of our time'), etc. — in which the rule of the finance aristocracy was denounced and stigmatized with greater or less wit. (*Ibid.*, pp. 196-197)

National feeling could only be unified and harnessed in the name of the July monarchy. Instead, the conservative foreign policy dictated by the finance houses gradually solidified national feeling against the existing regime, culminating in the effects of the political events in Europe of the years 1846-1848. Guizot, Louis Philippe's minister, had come out in favour of the Holy Alliance against the Swiss, and when the latter were victorious in 'this mimic war', this 'raised the self-respect of the bourgeois opposition in France'.

And then, given the explosive internal condition of the French nation, 'the bloody uprising of the people in Palermo (January 12, 1848) worked like an electric shock on the paralysed masses of the people and awoke their great revolutionary memories and passions.' Thus, given a certain level of the development of internal contradictions in French society, international events which at another time might have had little effect or even have been used to discourage political activity, could provide a major impetus to revolution.

Indeed, it was from the international level, but this time economically, that the revolutionary opposition's formation was finally completed and fused into a striking force. 'The eruption of the general discontent was finally accelerated and the sentiment for revolt ripened by two economic world events.' First came the potato blight and bad harvests of 1845-1846 and the consequent heightening of the glaring contrasts between the poverty of the masses and the unrestrained luxury of the finance aristocracy: 'At Buzançais the hunger rioters executed; in Paris the over-satiated *escrocs* (swindlers) snatched from the courts by the royal family.'

For Marx, this condition of a sharp reduction in living standards and even prolonged hunger enter as one of the conjunctural factors in building up the revolutionary situation, something which 'ripened the sentiment for revolt' and 'accelerated the general discontent'. Discussions about impoverishment and hunger as the 'causes' of revolution derive from an extreme vulgarization of Marx's views, and must be dismissed on that count if they are raised as criticisms of Marxian theory. For Marx, the whole preceding social and political development, determined in its main lines by the economic structure, prepares the disposition of class forces which enters into a revolutionary situation. From then on, the movement of events is subject to the laws and mechanisms of the political class struggle, and now the developments in the 'economic base' will have effects which are determined in this political framework. In 1846-1848, therefore, the growing impoverishment enters only secondarily, as a determinant of tempo and a contributory factor to the heightening of consciousness of already fashioned conflicting interests.

The second 'economic world event' of this order was 'a *general commercial and industrial crisis* in England'; and now Marx can describe the actual gathering of the revolutionary storm. All the factors he has considered are brought into action in the concrete course of events:

> The devastation of trade and industry caused by the economic epidemic made the autocracy of the finance aristocracy still more unbearable. Throughout the whole of France the bourgeois opposition evoked the broadest agitation for an electoral reform which should win for them the majority in the Chambers and overthrow the Ministry of the Bourse. In Paris the industrial crisis had, in particular, the result of throwing a number of manufacturers and big traders, who under the existing circumstances could no longer do any business in the foreign market, on to the home market. They set up large *épiciers* and *boutiquiers* en masse. Hence the innumerable bankruptcies among this section of the Paris bourgeoisie, and hence their revolutionary action in February. It is known how Guizot and the Chambers answered the reform proposals with a plain challenge, how Louis Philippe too late resolved on a Ministry led by Barrot, how hand-to-hand fighting took place between the people and the army, how the army was disarmed by the passive conduct of the National Guard, how the July monarchy had to give way to a Provisional government. (*Ibid.*, p. 198)

Marx and Engels considered afterwards that they made two errors in their evaluation of the 1848 revolutions. In the first place, they mistook the economic crisis of 1847-1848 for a manifestation of the impending collapse of the capitalist system, whereas that system proved beyond doubt to have within it great scope for the expansion of the productive forces, particularly with the growth of United States capitalism. The industrialization of Europe itself had only just begun, and at a later date Marx asked Engels in correspondence the question: even if we are successful in a socialist revolution in old Europe, where capitalism has matured, would we not risk defeat on a world scale of the still unfulfilled promise of capitalism in the rest of the world?

At any rate the return to economic 'normality' was the primary reason for the ebb of the revolutionary wave in Europe after 1848, and Marx and Engels found it necessary to fight hard against those elements in the revolutionary emigré groups who urged fresh revolutionary attempts. To these elements, Marx and Engels pointed out that they were ignoring everything gained by the Marxist conception and returning to Utopianism.

This is connected with Marx and Engels' second self-criticism over their analysis of 1848. They admitted themselves influenced by the predominance in French revolutionary history of small conspiratorial groups acting 'on behalf' of the working class or 'the people', a trend personified by Auguste Blanqui. After 1848 Marx and Engels devoted even more attention than before to the problems involved in the development of the consciousness of the working class itself, and the kind of organization and leadership necessary for this development. However heroic, disciplined and skilful the men making up the parties of the type led by Blanqui, and however much they kept the bourgeois awake in their beds at night, they could not achieve the kind of revolution necessary to overthrow capitalism. In this respect Marx and Engels were able to develop, to make more precise and definite, the picture of revolution which they had given in *The German Ideology*.

There they had already insisted that revolution is not an unfortunate necessity, a by-product of the transition to a classless society, but is the actual experience by which men change themselves through changing their own environment, thus producing 'communist consciousness' on 'a mass scale'. And in the 'Communist Manifesto' they say: 'The emancipation of the working class is the task of the working class itself.'

The meaning of this principle emerged more clearly from the experience of the 1848 revolutions and the light it shed on past revolutionary history. Groups of the Blanquist type tended to be isolated from the masses, devoting themselves to their own training and preparation, studying the enemy and awaiting the propitious occasion, instead of sinking roots into the mass movement, studying all the developments in the class struggle, and particularly the experience of the working class itself. Not only that, but there would tend to persist in such groups the notion that the seizure of power, the control of the existing system of government and state machine, was the political aim of the movement.

Marx's deduction from 1848, finally made precise, once again through a study of the actual historical experience of the working class in struggle, in the Paris Commune of 1871, was that the existing state machine must be *smashed*, and a proletarian dictatorship established, its organs class organs, its guiding principle to prepare its own historical redundancy and disappearance through drawing the masses into its work, a change made possible through the economic transformations of socialist construction, which at the same time removed the economic necessity for the state as organs of suppression of one class by another.

Class and revolution

The laws of the process of revolution, the relationship between party and class, the theory of the state and revolution, the nature of the transition to socialism — all of these are involved in understanding Marx's answer to the questions we outlined previously on the preconditions and nature of the 1848 events in France. This complexity is characteristic of Marx's approach to all such questions, and it is this which explains the importance in the history of Marxism of the disputes over 'revisionism' on all questions, philosophical, historical, economic, and political. Here we do not deal with the later development of these questions by Marxists, in which Lenin and Trotsky, in their writings on the international developments during and after the First World War, particularly relating to the Russian Revolution, provided brilliant examples of the method elaborated by Marx. (cf. especially Trotsky, *History of the Russian Revolution*, 3 vols., and Lenin, *Collected Works*.) Trotsky turns on numerous occasions to the relationship between fluctuations in economic prosperity and working class militancy and revolution. (cf. Trotsky, *The First Five Years of the Communist International*, 2 vols., and *Le Mouvement Communiste en France*, ed. P. Broué.)

As for the second self-criticism made by Marx and Engels, to expand on it would be to trace the development of Marxist thought for over a century, since the development of the proletarian revolution and revolutionary consciousness is, of course, the core of Marxism. Lenin's *State and Revolution* is the classic work on that aspect of the question which came to the fore in the second decade of the 20th century. His *What is to be Done?*, even though written as a pamphlet directed to a particular crisis in the Russian Social Democratic Party, is a development of the general principles involved in the other essential question: the relation between party and class, theory and practice.

Marx's analysis of the stages by which first the proletariat and then the revolutionary democracy of the petty bourgeoisie, followed by each more 'right' section of the opposition were defeated, is presented in brilliantly concise, concrete and graphic form in Marx's two books on the period, and this summary cannot be a substitute for the works themselves. The key to this process is in its first stage, the manifestation of the principal contradiction contained in the February victory. It was the proletariat which on the streets of Paris, established the new power, and there was no alternative to the pronouncement of a Republic with social emancipation inscribed on its banners. Respectable papers like the *Moniteur* '... had to propagate officially the "wild ravings" which up to that time lay buried in the apocryphal writings of the Socialists and only reached the ears of the bourgeoisie from time to time as remote, half terrifying, half-ludicrous legends.'

Since 'everyone' was prepared to identify the finance aristocracy with the enemy described in the socialist pamphlets, and since the bourgeois themselves were represented by ideologues whose explicit Republican programme attributed any class distinctions not to economic relations, but only to the effects of monarchy and aristocratic institutions, 'nobody' was against the 'emancipation of the proletariat' and the 'social republic'; and *fraternité* united all classes in a post-revolutionary euphoria. It was this air which the Provisional Government breathed ...for the duration of its very short life.

Marx's analysis shows that the necessities of bourgeois economy and particularly of the running of the state quickly made necessary a settlement with the extravagant promises given to the workers.

> The emancipation of the workers — even as a phrase — became an unbearable danger to the new republic, for it was a standing protest against the restoration of credit, which rests on undisturbed and untroubled recognition of the existing economic class relationships. Therefore, it was necessary to have done with the workers.

Twenty-four battalions of Mobile Guards were formed from the Paris *lumpenproletariat* in order to be turned against the working class, a working class which at first welcomed them as their own. The National Workshops were set up and took in 100,000 workers. In reality nothing but workhouses, they yet bore the same name as the 'Ateliers' campaigned for by the socialists and Louis Blanc, who was in any case a minister in the Provisional government. The way in which petty-bourgeois public opinion was rallied consequently against the working class showed a pattern which has often since then been repeated.

> All the discontent, all the ill-humour of the petty bourgeois was simultaneously directed against these National Ateliers, the common target. With real fury they reckoned up the sums that the proletarian loafers swallowed, while their own situation became daily more unbearable. A state pension

for sham labour, that is socialism! they growled to themselves. They sought the basis of their misery in the National Ateliers, the declarations of the Luxembourg, the marches of the workers through Paris. And no one was more fantastic about the alleged machinations of the Communists than the petty bourgeoisie who hovered hopelessly on the brink of bankruptcy.

In the months before the meeting of the new Assembly and the formal declaration of the Republic in May 1848, the working class continued to show its strength, but it went through no preparation equivalent to that of its enemy. The National Assembly of May now provoked the decisive struggle: to secure the republic for the bourgeoisie and to put the workers in their place. The proletariat's representatives were removed from all government bodies, and the proposal for a Labour Ministry was rejected.

On May 15, a workers' demonstration invaded the Assembly, attempting to call it to order, to the February order, but the only real result of this action was the arrest of Barbés, Blanqui and the other leaders. Next must come the settlement on the streets: if the workers' confidence derived from their predominance in the street battles of February, then they must be given a practical demonstration of the real relationship of forces. A series of provocative decrees and speeches in the Assembly forced the workers into the great insurrection and defeat of June 22, 1848: '. . . the first great battle between the two classes that split modern society. It was a fight for the preservation or annihilation of the bourgeois order. The veil that shrouded the republic was torn to pieces.'

Once the proletariat was defeated, the 'middle sections' or petty bourgeoisie came more easily under attack. Their misfortune was that, having chosen to attack the working class during the latter's period of strength, they were then forced to side with it only at the time of its defeat. The analysis of the role of the petty bourgeoisie in these events is one which retains validity as the guide to many subsequent historical situations. The powerlessness of this class derived from its middle position, tossed between the two great classes, victim always of its illusions about the good society of small and hardworking citizens like themselves, only disturbed by the inordinate strength and greed of the bourgeoisie on one side and the proletariat on the other.

The experience of the proletariat in these defeats, however, is of a different kind, a necessary experience in that the bourgeoisie must clarify in practice the meaning of its politics and the essence of its republican form of state, a *bourgeois* republic, explicitly disclaiming the 'social' republic of February. Thus Marx: 'By making its burial-place the birthplace of the bourgeois republic, the proletariat compelled the latter to come out forthwith in its pure form as the state whose admitted object is to perpetuate the rule of capital, the slavery of labour.'

Without here going into the later stages by which all the 'middle sections', and finally the democrats of the big bourgeoisie themselves, were defeated, we note one other result of the June defeat of the Paris proletariat. All over the rest of Europe, this demonstration of both the menace of the proletariat and the necessity of its suppression pushed the bourgeoisie into the arms of reaction as a 'lesser evil'. And in those nations where the February victory had sparked off democratic revolt against the Russian, Austrian and Prussian yokes, the old powers once again turned with confidence to the imposition of their rule, sure that 'revolutionary' France would this time be too concerned with the suppression of the proletariat at home to encourage revolution in eastern and central Europe: 'The Hungarian shall not be free, nor the Pole, nor the Italian, as long as the worker remains a slave!'

This was the essence of Marx's conclusions from the revolutions of 1848 and the defeat of the Paris proletariat: Until February 1848 the working class inevitably proceeded behind the banner of a revolution to change the form of the state. That state was the monopoly of the finance aristocracy, of one section of the bourgeoisie and its representatives. After June, the aim of the proletariat must be the social revolution, overthrow of the social-economic system, political independence of the proletariat, smashing of the bourgeois state, dictatorship of the proletariat: 'Our battle-cry must be: the permanent revolution!'

A Marxist view of any revolution would be of this type: i.e., not simply to provide an explanation of the classes and their roles, but to make this explanation from the standpoint of the enrichment of the experience and knowledge of the tasks of the working class, and of Marxism itself as the theory of the revolution of that class.

Before dealing with the closing chapter of the 1848 historical drama, viz., the accession to power of Louis Bonaparte, we must bring together certain of Marx's comments on class and ideology, since they are his most explicit statements on this subject (with the exception of *Capital* where specifically economic illusions are analysed).

Classes and their political ideologists.

> Upon the different forms of property, upon the social conditions of existence, rises an entire superstructure of distinct and characteristically formed sentiments, illusions, modes of thought and views of life. The entire class creates and forms them out of its material foundations and out of the corresponding social relations. The single individual who derives them through tradition and education may imagine that they form the real motives and starting point of his activity. (*The 18th Brumaire of Louis Bonaparte*, Selected Works, Vol. II, p. 344)

These general remarks are made by Marx by way of explanation of his insistence that the Legitimists and Orleanists were divided not only by their explicit attachment to different royal houses, but by the property relations which determined the lives of those making up the two groups: 'large landed proprietors, ruling through priests and lackeys', on the one hand; 'high finance, large-scale industry, wholesale trade, i.e., capital, governed with its retinue of lawyers, professors and orators', on the other.

The fact that loyalty to one or the other royal house predominates in the *conscious* motives of individual representatives of the class, that a whole political party takes its decisions according to the degree of fervour aroused from time to time on this question, does not alter the fact that the royal houses are only titles for class groupings, forms by which the class interest is held together for certain purposes, but not the determinant of the content and social composition of the groups, despite a number of accidental adherents attached purely by loyalty to the dynasty. These different sections of the ruling class will under some circumstances (degree of strength of the opposed class, etc.) draw closer together and even merge their material interests and their ideological outlooks.

Two general points are important in this context: firstly, the conformity of the whole ideological superstructure with the economic base is a process, working through the survival of older historical forms of thought represented in the lives of certain classes: secondly, the individual ideologists have their own unique experiences and starting points in politics, but they make this experience in the matrix of conditions common to their class, with its characteristic emphasis within the ideology of the society. The individual will tend to regard the ideological expressions of his class interests as his own 'real' starting point, since that is in fact where he starts, but the material class interests themselves, and the impetus they give to a particular emphasis within the ideology of the society, create the ideological conditions within which the individual works at his ideas.

Marx gives the example of the petty bourgeoisie. It cannot break from the rule of the bourgeoisie or challenge any of its basic categories, but its class position leads it always at the general interests of society, of 'the people'. The content of its policies is:

> ... the transformation of society in a democratic way, but a transformation within the bounds of the petty bourgeoisie. Only one must not form the notion that the petty bourgeoisie, on principle, wishes to enforce an egoistic class interest. Rather, it believes that the special conditions of its emancipation are the *general* conditions under which modern society can alone be saved and the class struggle avoided. Just as little must one imagine that the democratic representatives are all shopkeepers or enthusiastic champions of shopkeepers. According to their education and their individual position they may be separated from them as widely as heaven from earth. What makes them representatives of the petty bourgeoisie is the fact that in their minds they do not go beyond the limits which the latter do not go beyond in life, that they are consequently driven theoretically to the same tasks and solutions to which material interest and social position practically drive the latter. This is in general the relationship of the political and literary representatives of a class to the class that they represent. (*Ibid.*, p. 347)

A sort of process of 'selection' is involved, rather than the direct 'production' by each class of its own ideological representatives. Here Marx issues his own corrective in advance against any temptation to apply mechanically his formulation in relation to the Orleanists and Legitimists, quoted earlier, and occurring only three pages before passages we have just cited at length. Such ideological representatives of the class must not be mistaken for the class itself, which is held together by its particular historical basis in property in the means of production. Marx brings this home in describing the phase following the defeat of the June 1848 insurrection. Now the bourgeoisie must consolidate its rule, first through raising its 'Republican' political representatives to the head of state, and then liquidating these same bourgeois Republicans. These politicians, with their organ the *National*, had formed the official opposition under Louis Philippe. Their political programme was 'realized', in the sense that June 1848 brought them into office, but in a manner determined by the real play of class forces and not at all by their own idea of how they would attain political office. Thus their political illusions fitted them very well for the specific role required by the bourgeoisie after June 1848, but only because they were real victims of these illusions:

> The republican bourgeois section, which had long regarded itself as the legitimate heir of the July monarchy, thus found itself successful beyond its hopes; it attained power, however, not as it had dreamed under Louis Phillippe, through a liberal revolt of the bourgeoisie against the throne, but through a rising of the proletariat against capital, a rising laid low with grape-shot. What it had pictured to itself as the most revolutionary happening turned out in reality to be the most counter-revolutionary. The fruit fell into its lap, but it fell from the tree of knowledge, not from the tree of life. (*Ibid.*, pp. 327-328)

In this relation between a class and its political representatives we have a striking illustration of the relation between 'being and consciousness' which dominates the earlier writings of Marx. The French bourgeoisie as a class is involved in the making of history through the totality of its relations with other classes (particularly the proletariat) and its internal relations: these again are part of the development of world capitalism, including the completion of capitalism's progressive struggle against the remnants of feudal absolutism (as we saw in Marx's analysis of the foreign relations of the 1848 Republic and the consequences of the June insurrection's defeat).

The conscious representatives of the class, however, do not develop their ideas, programmes and policies on the basis of a direct and total translation of all these relationships. Knowledge always represents only an approximation to reality, and in this case only through the specifically political relationships which the parties take to be their life-substance; this in addition to the fact that ideological, non-scientific thinking always takes as its material the historically given and does not penetrate to the preconditions and processes which produced that 'given' and prepare its dissolution. When rapid changes take place in the life of a class, as in the torrent of 1848, or in the undetected developments at the economic base of society, the political representatives of the class will tend to persist in the framework of ideas in which they have always worked. They are not the class itself, and are not immediately subject to all the changes affecting the life of the class; on the contrary, they play a specific role, a political role, in the 'division of labour' within the class.

At times (June 1848) this very conviction of the self-contained character of their own principles fits them for a dominant historical role, though, as we have seen, not the way they expect. At other times (1849-1850) they pay the penalty of their ideas being tied in the past. What was this republican section of the bourgeoisie?

> Under the bourgeois monarchy of Louis Philippe it had formed the official Republican opposition and consequently a recognized, component part of the political world of the day. It had its representatives in the Chamber and a considerable sphere of influence in the press. Its Paris organ, the *National*, was considered just as respectable in its way as the *Journal des Débats*. Its character corresponded to this position under the constitutional monarchy. It was not a section of the bourgeoisie held together by great, common interests and marked off by specific conditions of production. (*Ibid.*, p. 326)

In combination with our earlier quotations from Marx on class and ideology (*The Materialist Conception of History*) these remarks must suffice. In general, Marx's writings on 1848 remain the finest exposition of this relationship. What was in his polemic against Proudhon a theoretical explanation of the class source of petty-bourgeois ideology here becomes concrete in the history of the vacillating role of these middle strata in a revolution, covered over always with their tendency to earnestly express their own class interests in the guise of solutions for society as a whole. One of the prime conclusions drawn by Marx from the 1848 experience was the need for the proletariat to strive for its complete political independence from the petty bourgeoisie.

Only on that basis would individuals or sections from the petty bourgeoisie then attach themselves politically to the proletariat. Marx and Engels carried this fight into German Social-Democracy to the end of their lives.

1848 provided for Marx a living fulfilment of his characterization of the type of social and economic reform put forward by Proudhon as 'petty-bourgeois'. Now the petty bourgeoisie moved to the acceptance of already outdated Utopian socialist schemes, as it sought for some way to express its specific complaint against capitalism:

> Capital hounds this class chiefly as its *creditors,* so it demands *credit institutions;* capital crushes it by *competition,* so it demands *associations* supported by the state; capital overwhelms it by *concentration,* so it demands *progressive taxes,* limitations on inheritance, taking over a large growth by the state, and other measures that forcibly stem the growth of capital. Since it dreams of the peaceful achievement of its socialism — allowing, perhaps, for a second February lasting a brief day — naturally

the coming historical process appears to it as the application of systems, which the thinkers of society, whether in companies or as individual inventors, devise or have devised. Thus they become the eclectics and adepts of the existing socialist systems, of *doctrinaire socialism*, which was the theoretical expression of the proletariat only so long as it had not yet developed further into a free historical self-movement.

Experience at the same time gave the proletariat a sense of its own 'free historical self-movement', and 'the proletariat rallies more and more round *revolutionary socialism*, round *communism*, for which the bourgeoisie has itself found the name of Blanqui. This socialism is the declaration of the permanence of the revolution, *the class dictatorship* of the proletariat as the inevitable transit point to the *abolition of class differences generally etc.*' (Marx, *The Class Struggles in France 1848-1850*, Selected Works Vol. II, pp. 288-289)

1848: the bourgeoisie and the democratic state

Marx's earliest political writings had been concerned with explaining that the state, the sphere of politics, was the product of social relations and not their creator, and that, far from being the guarantor and embodiment of social unity and peace, it was the expression of the irreconcilability of social antagonisms. We have seen that 1848 enabled Marx to go much further: he reached the historic conclusion that the proletariat cannot simply transfer into its own hands the bureaucratic military machine of the state, but must 'smash' it and develop its own organs of state power. But the same historical turning-point which enabled Marx to make this theoretical conclusion for the proletarian revolution also posed a special problem for the relationship between the bourgeoisie and the democratic state, and the interrelation between these two problems was to prove the motive force in the political developments of the ensuing century. So threatening was the strength of the working class that the bourgeoisie everywhere turned, after 1848, to a compromise with reaction. Of course, the economic impact of capitalism's continuing expansion was still fundamentally revolutionary: in opening up new markets and breaking up old social systems; in dissolving old social forms within the capitalist countries; in developing the productive forces; in concentrating and increasing the force of the proletariat.

But politically 1848 was a major turning of the ways. We take up here two aspects of this historical watershed which are of great value in illustrating the method of Marx in understanding social and political relations as fundamentally relations of class struggle: the connection between the ruling class in Marx's sense (the propertied class, in this case the bourgeoisie) and government; and the precise analysis of the role of the small peasantry in the accession to power of Louis Bonaparte.

At the very point, in 1848, where the French bourgeoisie found it necessary to remove the sectional interests which restricted its full development through control of the July monarchy — a removal which took a *Republican-democratic form,* capable of momentarily uniting all classes beneath it — it was forced to engage in a political struggle with the proletariat which rendered this Republican democracy still-born, with similar consequences throughout Europe. The right-wing Party of Order, after the June 1848 insurrection, took the opportunity of branding as 'socialist' every democratic measure proposed in the assembly. Marx comments:

> This was not merely a figure of speech, fashion or party tactics. The bourgeoisie had true insight into the fact that all the weapons which it had forged against feudalism turned their points against itself, that all the means of education which it had produced rebelled against its own civilization, that all the gods which it had created had fallen away from it. It understood that all the so-called bourgeois liberties and organs of progress attacked and menaced its class rule at its social foundation and its political summit simultaneously, and had therefore become 'socialistic' ... What the bourgeoisie did not grasp, however, was the logical conclusion that its *own parliamentary regime,* that its *political rule* in general, was now bound to meet with the general verdict of being likewise *socialistic.* As long as the rule of the bourgeois class had not been organized completely, as long as it had not acquired its pure political expression, the antagonism of the other classes likewise could not appear in its pure form, and where it did appear, could not take the dangerous turn that transforms every struggle against the power of the state into a struggle against capital. (*The 18th Brumaire,* Selected Works Vol. II, pp. 361-362)

And because of this, the bourgeoisie has to be 'delivered from the danger of *governing in its own name'.* The deliverance was carried out by Louis Bonaparte, resting on the small peasantry.

It is interesting once again to note that Marx attempts always to explain the *necessity* of every major historical experience, and does not write history as a series of mistakes and inspirations. Not a theory worked out as predictions in advance, but the experience of the 1848 struggle and the abortive republic, was necessary to bring into the life of the bourgeoisie the realization of the great historical turning-point marked by the political baptism of its evil opposite and inescapable familiar, the proletariat. Only these experiences, reverberating through the life of the whole class and its surrounding petty-bourgeois strata, could establish the meaning of the new stage in history.

It is this changed *class* content of the 1848 revolution which explains its different course from that of 1789, and which confounds the search for a regular series of stages by the few historians and sociologists who have attempted explanations of 'the revolutionary phenomenon'.

> In the first French Revolution the rule of the Constitutionalists is followed by the rule of the Girondins and the rule of the Girondins by the rule of the Jacobins. Each of these parties supported itself on the more progressive party. As soon as it has brought the revolution far enough to be unable to follow it further, still less to go ahead of it, it is thrust aside by the bolder ally that stands behind it and sent to the guillotine. The revolution thus moves along an ascending line.
>
> It is the reverse with the Revolution of 1848. The proletarian party appears as an appendage of the petty-bourgeois democratic party. It is betrayed and dropped by the latter on April 16, May 15, and in the June days. The democratic party, in its turn, leans on the shoulders of the bourgeois-Republican party. The bourgeois-republicans no sooner believe themselves well established than they shake off the troublesome comrade and support themselves on the shoulders of the Party of Order.
>
> The Party of Order hunches its shoulders, lets the bourgeois-Republicans tumble and throws itself on the shoulders of the armed force. It fancies it is still sitting on its shoulders when, one fine morning, it perceives that the shoulders have transformed themselves into bayonets. Each party strikes from behind at that pressing further and leans from in front on that pressing back. No wonder that in this ridiculous posture it loses its balance and, having made the inevitable grimaces, collapses with curious capers. The revolution thus moves in a descending line. (*Ibid.*, pp. 339-340.)

In an important sense, the history of France since 1848 is the history of the French bourgeoisie's inability to find any permanent form of political rule for the protection of its class domination. Again and again, 'the Party of Order' must rear its head, restriction of democracy becomes necessary, revolutionary traditions once again are resurgent in the working class, a new Bonaparte is sought. Undoubtedly however the predominant factor in any analysis of

French politics today would now be, taking into account the national and international economic and political developments over the century, the crisis of consciousness and leadership in the proletariat resulting from its experience of betrayal, rather than the historical role of the bourgeoisie.

German history presents the same phenomenon in even more brutal form; and the best way to conclude and summarize this section is to quote at length Engels' famous verdict on the politics of German capitalism, some of the most prophetic words ever written:

> The misfortune of the German bourgeoisie is that in the favourite German manner it arrived too late. The period of its ascendancy occurs at a time when the bourgeoisie of the other W. European countries is already politically in decline . . .
>
> It is a peculiarity of the bourgeoisie, distinguishing it from all former ruling classes, that there is a turning point in its development after which every further increase in its means of power, that is in the first place every increase of its capital, only tends to make it more and more incapable of ruling politically.
>
> '*Behind the big bourgeois stand the proletarians.*' To the extent that the bourgeoisie develops its industry, its commerce and its means of communication, to the same extent it also produces the proletariat. And at a certain point — which need not appear everywhere at the same time or at the same stage of development — it begins to notice that this, its proletarian double, is outgrowing it. From that moment on, it loses the power for exclusive political domination; it looks round for allies with whom it shares its domination, or to whom it cedes its whole domination, as circumstances may demand.
>
> In Germany this turning point came for the bourgeoisie as early as 1848. And actually the German bourgeoisie was frightened not so much by the German as by the French proletariat. The June battle in Paris, in 1848, showed the bourgeoisie what it had to expect; the German proletariat was just restless enough to make it clear that the seed of the same harvest had been sown in German soil also; and from that day on the edge was taken off all bourgeois political action. The bourgeoisie looked round for allies, bargained itself away to them regardless of price — and even today it is not a step further forward. (*Selected Works*, Vol. II, pp. 537-538)

The consequence, as Engels noted four years later in amending the same 'prefatory note' to his *The Peasant War in Germany*, was this: 'Thus it has been the peculiar fate of Prussia to complete its bourgeois revolution, begun in 1803 to 1813 and advanced further in 1848, in the peasant form of Bonapartism at the end of this century.' (*Ibid.*)

At this point, Engels cites his own earlier remarks in 'The Housing Question', which adequately refute any suggestion that for Marxist theory the governing personnel are identical with the ruling class:

> But both in the old absolute monarchy and in the modern Bonapartist monarchy, the real governing power lies in the hands of a special caste of army officers and state officials. In Prussia this caste is supplemented partly from its own ranks, partly from the lesser aristocracy owning the entailed estates, more rarely the higher aristocracy and least of all from the bourgeoisie. The independence of this caste, which appears to occupy a position outside and, so to speak, above society, gives the state the semblance of independence in relation to society. (*Ibid.*, p. 544)

Also important in this context are the articles by Marx on the political parties and government in England, in which he demonstrates the way in which the English bourgeoisie accepts the aristocratic landed families as the legitimate occupants of government office [cited in Bottomore and Rubel, *Karl Marx, Selected Writings in Sociology and Social Philosophy*, pp. 191-200] Engels even remarked in one of his letters that he was coming round to the conclusion that 'the bourgeoisie has not the stuff in it for ruling directly itself', so far was he from a mechanical theory of ruling class and state power. In England the bourgeoisie would pay the oligarchy to do the work, but elsewhere 'a Bonapartist semi-dictatorship in the normal form'. (Letter to Marx, April 13, 1866.)

Marx and Engels recognized that Parliamentary democracy, with its highly generalized and abstract notion of the citizen's rights, is the political equivalent of the bourgeois everyday economic order (not of its basic production relations), and therefore the ideology of capitalism's most consistent political representatives in the period of its growth and positive contribution to progress. But at the same time they devoted more attention to the class struggle produced by the production relations, whose intensity and whose dialectic rudely disrupted all possibility of the attainment of the bourgeois political ideal except in rare and transitory circumstances. 1848 was a watershed made by the practical class struggle against all existing political 'principles'. This historical change was reflected scientifically only in that theory which begins from the struggle of classes rooted in property in the means of production, Marxism. The class actions of 1848 thus did not only 'confirm' a theory; they enriched and advanced it, and made it possible for it to go on to grasp the actually changed situation produced by these actions.

These 'theoretical' conclusions are again not separate from political ones. Once grasped, they make possible a revolutionary strategy which goes beyond all the varieties of radicalism, including those 'socialist' varieties which declare as their aim the unity of all true 'democrats' around the working class. What 1848 showed was that, the greater the political independence and strength of the working class, the more imperative the turn of the bourgeoisie and those tied to it to anti-democracy, to counter-revolution. The history of the socialist movement is littered with the political corpses of those who rejected this lesson, and tailored their programme to what suited the 'democrats', i.e. the petty bourgeoisie. The disasters attendant on this abandonment of the political independence of the working class were most brutally demonstrated in the rise of fascism in the 1930s.

The peasants

We have already taken Marx's well-known definition of the small peasantry as 'a class and not a class' to illustrate his views on the relation between the economic and political processes in a class's formation. Equally instructive is his explanation of how this very amorphous character of the peasantry, given their history since the decrees following the Revolution of 1789, laid the basis for the power of Louis Napoleon. Marx's classic text *The 18th Brumaire of Louis Bonaparte*, besides constituting a model of the method of historical materialism, throws much light on the subsequently vexed and momentous problem of the relationship of the peasantry to the socialist revolution. For example, Lenin's strategy in Russia did not include the 'peasant alliance' simply as an organizational device, but was the extension into the conditions of backward Russia of the theoretical conclusions of Marx and Engels from 1848 and in the subsequent years.

> The Bonaparte dynasty (writes Marx) represents not the revolutionary, but the conservative peasant; not the peasant that strikes out beyond the condition of his social existence, the small holding, but rather the peasant who wants to consolidate it; not the country folk who want to overthrow the old order through their own energies linked up with the towns, but on the contrary those who, in stupefied bondage to this old order, want to see themselves with their small-holding saved and favoured by the ghost of the empire. It represents not the enlightenment, but the superstition of the

peasant; not his judgement, but his prejudice: not his future, but his past: not his modern Cavennes [where a famous peasant uprising took place in the early 18th century] but his modern Vendée [where the peasants supported the Royalists after 1789] (*The 18th Brumaire*, Selected Works, Vol. II, p. 416)

In the years of the parliamentary republic of 1848 up to the *coup d'état* of Louis Napoleon in December 1851, 'the modern and the traditional consciousness of the French peasant contended for mastery'. Marx's method here should be noted. He does not deduce the political character of the peasant 'once and for all' from the economic-social definition of the class, but sees upon this basis a struggle between 'the past and the future' of the peasants as a class, a struggle joined only through the drawing of the peasants into the maelstrom of political history from 1848 to 1851, which had already been explained by Marx as the outcome of economic and class developments at the national and international levels (above). This development 'from the outside' sets the terms under which the struggle of past against future in the peasantry takes place, and *on this basis* Marx discusses the disputes over local government, education, religion, morality, and so on, which raged among the peasants. This method should be contrasted with any pseudo-Marxist 'analyses' which build up some 'model' of the class psychology of the peasant (or of the bourgeois, etc.) from the material conditions of his existence and then proceed to test it, confirm it, refine it, etc., through a consideration of various facts about peasant life and peasant history.

Attempts to present 'working-class culture' by a similar method, instead of through the historical analysis of the central experiences of the proletariat's struggle to become a 'class for itself' in conflict with the bourgeoisie, prove still more ludicrous. This struggle between the past and the future of the peasantry is not to be understood just as a matter of consciousness, or as some tragic fate. Its material basis is made clear in the brilliant closing passages of *The 18th Brumaire*, particularly in the following paragraphs (pp. 417-418):

> After the first revolution (1789) had transformed the peasants from semi-villeins into freeholders, Napoleon confirmed and regulated the conditions on which they could exploit undisturbed the soil of France which had just come into their possession and slake their youthful passion for property. But what is now causing the ruin of the French peasant is his dwarf holding itself, the division of the land, the form of property which Napoleon consolidated in France. It is precisely the material conditions

which made the feudal peasant into a small peasant and Napoleon into an emperor. Two generations have sufficed to produce the inevitable result: progressive deterioration of agriculture, progressive indebtedness of the agriculturist.

The 'Napoleonic' form of property, which at the beginning of the 19th century was the condition for the liberation and enrichment of the French countryfolk, has developed in the course of this century as the law of their enslavement and pauperisation. And it is just this law which is the first of the *idées napoléoniennes* which the second Bonaparte has to uphold.

If he still shares with the peasants the illusion that the cause of their ruin is to be sought not in this small-holding property itself but outside it in the influence of secondary causes, then his experiments will burst like soap bubbles when they come into contact with the relations of production.

Marx goes on to show how the small-holding, the extension of private property of the bourgeois type into the countryside, which had been the main guarantee of the bourgeois order against feudal restoration, had within two generations turned into the new enslavement of the small peasant:

> The bourgeois order, which at the beginning of the century set the state to stand guard over the newly-arisen small-holding and manured it with laurels, has become a vampire that sucks out its blood and marrow and throws them into the alchemistic cauldrons of capital. The *Code Napoleon* is now nothing but a codex of distraints, forced sales and compulsory auctions.

The *future* interests of the peasantry are therefore only to be found in the overthrow of the bourgeois order, and in alliance with that social force which can overthrow it, the proletariat. In so far as the peasantry remains the slave of its past, of its illusions of the permanent and prosperous small-holding, protected by the Emperor, its class nature will serve to strengthen the bourgeois state in its most repressive forms against the proletariat and the revolutionary sections of the peasantry itself. Thus:

> Besides the mortgage which capital imposes on it, the small-holding is burdened by taxes. Taxes are the source of life for the bureaucracy, the army, the priests and the court, in short, for the whole apparatus of the executive power. Strong government and heavy taxes are identical.
>
> By its very nature, small-holding property forms a suitable basis for all-powerful and innumerable bureaucracy.
>
> It creates a uniform level of relationships and persons over the whole surface of the land. Hence it also permits of uniform action from a supreme

centre on all points of this uniform mass. It annihilates the aristocratic intermediate grades between the mass of the people and the state power. On all sides, therefore, it calls forth the direct interference of this state power and the intervention of its immediate organs. (*Ibid.*, pp. 419-420)

Whereas the first Napoleon, in the 1790s, could take his revolutionary armies beyond France's borders and 'repay with interest' the taxes of the peasants through the opening up of vast new markets and the plunder of other nations, the second 'ghost' of the Empire needed to equip and pay his bureaucratic caste directly out of the state revenue from taxes; raising parasitism to new heights, if the expression is suitable.

Not only the state, but the Church also, is now placed in a position where it appears openly as the ideological protector of the ruin and oppression of the small peasant, rather than the religious accompaniment of his new-found independence, as in the 1790s. Finally the army, the last *idée napoléonienne*, which was after 1789 the flower of the peasant youth, becomes under Louis Napoleon 'the swamp-flower of the peasant *lumpenproletariat*'.

The development of capitalism between 1789 and 1848, the unfolding of its internal class conflicts just at the point where the bourgeoisie was forced to face up to its own last 'republican' struggle (1848), the maturing of new relations of production in society as a whole which imperiously demand the demise of the peasant small-holding — all this has built up 'behind the back' of the peasant a situation in which his traditional ideology is brought into complete contradiction with his material conditions of life, where every action into which he is forced will either confirm his oppression in still more bestial forms or, by a leap in consciousness through alliance with the proletariat, set going the process that will abolish his own and all private property.

Marx was wrong in his estimate of the stage of maturity for socialist revolution reached by French society in 1848. And yet, from his historical materialist analysis of these events he cast a searchlight on to the developing class relations of the capitalist system as a whole, and not only in France. It was 20 years before the ghost of Bonaparte was laid; but then, in 1871, in the action of thousands of workers in the Paris Commune who had certainly never read Marx, the final words of his *18th Brumaire* were dramatically and literally fulfilled: 'But if the imperial mantle finally falls on the shoulders of Louis Bonaparte, the iron statue of Napoleon will crash from the top of the Vendome column.'

It remains to explain the political consciousness and role of the peasantry in terms of our earlier presentation of the role of ideology. When Marx talks about 'false consciousness' he is not dismissing the ideological aspects of history as ephemeral. This 'false consciousness' must be understood as a *necessary* link in the causal chain, but the very conditions which make possible the recognition of its *falseness* as well as its necessity demand at the same time a struggle against its persistence. Marx concludes, on the illusions of the peasants:

> One sees: all *idées napoléoniennes* are the ideas of the undeveloped smallholding in the freshness of its youth; for the small-holding that has outlived its day they are an absurdity. They are only the hallucinations of its death struggle, words that are reduced to phrases, spirits reduced to ghosts.
>
> But the parody of imperialism was necessary to free the mass of the French nation from the weight of tradition and to work out in pure form the opposition between the state power and society. (*Ibid.*, p. 422)

And it was in the Paris Commune of 1871, 20 years later, that the proletariat made its first revolutionary bid against this 'pure form' of the bourgeois state. Paris was then isolated, particularly from the peasants in the countryside, but this time, in contrast with 1848, the proletariat discovered in practice that the old state machine must be *smashed*, and new independent organs of a new type of state be set up by the working class.

The question of revolutionary leadership based on Marxist theory and its need to project a strategy towards the peasantry among all its other tasks, was also posed by the Paris Commune, but because the 'parody' of 1851 had been lived through and exhausted, by 1871 qualitatively new experiences could be made. Marx wrote to Kugelmann: 'Whatever the immediate results may be, a new point of departure of world-historic importance has been gained'. (April 17, 1871.)

A note on 'the middle classes'

Under the general heading of 'the middle classes', many very different questions are often thrown together, with the purpose of suggesting that Marx's division 'proletariat-bourgeoisie' and his insistence on the polarization between these two classes, with the revolutionary consequences flowing from it, is misguided because it fails to account for the effect of intermediate and transitional layers or classes.

We have already seen that Marx's major work, *Capital*, is in any case concerned with a level of analysis where these intermediate layers are explicitly excluded from consideration.

At the political and ideological levels, however, the role of these middle strata is of great importance. In this chapter, for example, we have summarized the verdict of Marx on the role of the peasantry in the course of the last stages of the bourgeois revolution and its juncture with the first appearance of the revolutionary proletariat in 1848.

Obviously this has been a matter of political importance to the working-class movement ever since.

We confine ourselves here simply to indicating, with selected quotations from a great many which could be used, that Marx, Engels and their followers were keenly aware of the 'middle classes' problem, and that Marx's reference to it as 'irrelevant to present purposes' in *Capital* was not an isolated afterthought. Marx always discusses the problem, however, strictly in relation to the framework of the principal class conflict in the given society, that derived from the relations of production the key sectors of the mode of production. Referring to Ricardo, for example, he says:

> What Ricardo forgets to mention is the continual increase in numbers of the middle classes ...situated midway between the workers on one side and the capitalists and landowners on the other. These middle classes rest with all their weight upon the working class and at the same time increase the social security and power of the upper class. (*Theories of Surplus Value*. Cited in Bottomore and Rubel, *op. cit.*, p. 190)

Marxists would make a characterization of the economic basis and political role of each component part of these middle classes, with the first and obvious differentiation between 'new' middle classes based on the professional functionaries of the business corporations and state institutions and 'old' middle classes based on small business enterprise. But these classes are not fundamental in the sense of the 'economic law of motion' of capitalism. They enter the analysis at the level of struggle between the classes in all its aspects; this is why Marx draws attention to their 'pressure' on the proletariat and their function as an adjunct of the power of the bourgeoisie. Similarly, discussing an aspect of what is nowadays called 'social mobility' (i.e. the movement of individuals between social classes), Marx emphasises the relation of such social changes to the overall power-situation between the two main classes. Only from this standpoint can we ascertain the significance of the 'mobility':

> Although this situation continually brings an unwelcome number of new soldiers into the field, and into competition with the existing individual capitalists, it also consolidates the rule of capital itself, enlarges its basis, and enables it to recruit ever new forces for itself out of the lower layers of society. . .
>
> The more a ruling class is able to assimilate the most prominent men of the dominated classes the more stable and dangerous is its rule. (Kautsky, *Bernstein und das Socialdemokratische programm: eine antikritik*)

It is clear that the use of phrases like 'insurmountable class barriers' as indications of Marx's view of class by bourgeois sociologists like Lipset and Schumpeter amounts to gross misrepresentation. The question is not one of the fate of individuals or of the numbers of such individuals but of the changes in class relations. Later Marxists have taken account of the rise of the 'new' middle classes in exactly this way. These social groups were the subject of much discussion in the Marxist movement before the turn of the century. Lenin's review (1899) of Kautsky's reply to the 'revisionism' of Bernstein indicates the terms of the discussion. Lenin wrote:

> The chapter on the 'new middle estate' is likewise extremely interesting and, for us Russians, particularly instructive. If Bernstein had merely wanted to say that in place of the declining petty producers a new middle estate, the intelligentsia, is appearing, he would be perfectly correct, says Kautsky, pointing out that he himself noted the importance of this phenomenon several years before.
>
> In all spheres of people's labour, capitalism increases the number of office and professional workers with particular rapidity, and makes a growing demand for intellectuals. The latter occupy a special position among the other classes, attaching themselves partly to the bourgeoisie by their connections, their outlooks, etc., and partly to the wage-workers as capitalism increasingly deprives the intellectual of his independent position, converts him into a hired worker and threatens to lower his living standard. The transitory, unstable, contradictory position of that stratum of society now under discussion is reflected in the particularly widespread diffusion in its midst of hybrid, eclectic views, a farrago of contrasting principles and ideas, an urge to rise verbally to the higher spheres and to conceal conflicts between the historical groups of the population with phrases — all of which Marx lashed with his sarcasm half a century ago. (*Collected Works*, Vol. IV, pp. 201-202)

Three years later, Lenin drew attention to the relationship between this new middle estate and the old type of petty bourgeoisie, this time along the lines of Marx's note about the latter's 'pressure' on the proletariat:

> In all the countries of Europe, Russia included, the petty bourgeoisie is steadily being 'thrust to the wall' and falling into decline, a process which does not always express itself in the outright and direct elimination of the petty bourgeoisie, but in most cases leads to a reduction of its role in economic life, to deterioration of its living conditions, and greater insecurity.
>
> Everything militates against it: technical progress in big industrial and agricultural enterprises, the development of the big shops, the growth of manufactures' associations, cartels and trusts, and even the growth of consumers' societies and municipal enterprises. And, while the petty bourgeoisie is being 'thrust to the wall' in the sphere of agriculture and industry, a 'new middle social-estate', as the Germans say, is emerging and developing, a new stratum of the petty bourgeoisie, the intelligentsia, who are also finding life in capitalist society harder and harder and for the most part regard this society from the viewpoint of the small producer.
>
> It is quite natural that this must inevitably lead to widespread dissemination and constant revival of petty-bourgeois ideas and doctrines in the most varied forms. (*Ibid.*, Vol. VI, p.434)

Trotsky wrote in a similar vein about the political relations between these two social strata: 'The Socialist Party (of France) is not a working-class party either with regard to its policies or its social composition. It is the party of the new middle estate (the functionaries, civil servants, etc.) and, in part, of the petty bourgeoisie and the labour aristocracy.' (*Whither France*, p. 142)

In his *History of the Russian Revolution*, Trotsky, far from dismissing this 'new middle estate' as irrelevant, gives it a very important political role in the revolution:

> Lenin described Sukhanov as one of the best representatives of the petty bourgeoisie, and that is the most flattering thing that can be said of him.
>
> Only in this connection it must not be forgotten that the question is here of a new capitalist type of petty bourgeoisie, of industrial, commercial and bank clerks, the functionaries of capital on one side, and the workers' bureaucracy on the other — that is of that new middle caste, in whose name the well known German social democrat Edward Bernstein undertook at the end of the last century a revision of the revolutionary conceptions of Marx. (pp. 184-185)

According to Trotsky, this 'new middle caste', by reason particularly of its incorporation of a section of the bureaucracy grown up within the working class, has a unique political role:

> In order to answer the question how a revolution of workers and peasants came to surrender the power to the bourgeoisie (in Russia after February 1917), it is necessary to introduce into the political chain an intermediate link: the petty-bourgeois democrats and socialists of the Sukhanov type, journalists and politicians of the new middle caste, who had taught the masses that the bourgeoisie is an enemy, but themselves feared more than any thing else to release the masses from the control of that enemy.
>
> The contradiction between the character of the revolution and the character of the power that issued from it, is explained by the contradictory character of this new petty-bourgeois partition wall between the revolutionary masses and the capitalist bourgeoisie.

Trotsky also suggests that the failure of the German revolution of 1918-1919 can be laid at the door of the same social elements. The 'paradox' by which state power is handed back to the bourgeoisie by professed socialists, he says: '. . . seems all the more striking, because the experience of the German revolution of 1918 did not then exist, and humanity had not yet witnessed a colossal and still more successful operation of this same type carried out by the "new middle caste" led by the German social democracy.'

In the 1930s, Trotsky made a further contribution to the 'political sociology' of these middle strata in his analyses of the Nazi movement (*Germany: What Next?*). By the 1930s, it was not simply a matter of its representatives dominating and misleading the working-class movement, but rather a question of all the 'middle' sections, new and old, providing the mass basis for the counter-revolutionary forces mobilized by Hitler.

Central to all these examples is the need for a specific historical analysis in each case of the actual constituents of the 'middle classes' the actual extent to which their interests diverge or temporarily coalesce — all taken in relation to the main determinant of the political relationship of forces, the historic struggle between the two great classes in modern production: bourgeoisie and proletariat.

VI
Ideology and political economy in Marx's *Capital*

> In so far as Political Economy remains within that [bourgeois] horizon, in so far, i.e., as the capitalist regime is looked upon as the absolutely final form of social production, instead of as a passing historical phase of its evolution, Political Economy can remain a science only so long as the class struggle is latent or manifests itself only in isolated or sporadic phenomena. (Marx. Preface to the 2nd Edition (1873) of *Capital*, Vol. I.)

'Capital' and the Marxist theory of knowledge

Understanding Marx's method in *Capital* demands first of all that this historical verdict on 'political economy' be understood. If it is not, then the economic and social phenomena of capitalism are taken as manifestations of laws akin to laws of nature. Ricardo, for example, was able to recognize the antagonism of classes based on their economic interests, but was taken to task by Marx for 'naively taking this antagonism for a social law of nature'. When Marx says in his preface to the first edition (1867) that in his method 'the evolution of the economic formation of society is viewed as a process of natural history', he is stressing the objective and historical character of the process; his reference to Ricardo shows that *only* in so far as this historical aspect is given precedence can the distinctive character of social processes be understood. History, for Marx, is the process of man *becoming* man through a succession of modes of production, his own creations. Marx's theory of historical materialism summarized the nature of the contradictions which have effected the transitions between these successive modes. *Capital* is the test of this theory in the specific case of the capitalist mode of production. Ricardo's limitations were rooted in the fact that he produced his work in a period when the struggle of classes in capitalism was still not a generalized phenomenon with the force to pose the question of the overthrow of capitalism. Political Economy itself was the scientific reflection of that period; in his 'critique of political economy', Marx set himself the task of the conscious, scientific reflection of the rise of the working-class struggle to overthrow capitalism. Marx's economic-social categories are deliberate reflections of this struggle and the heightening of contradictions which it produces. The totality of these contradictions is grasped only by the most serious and thorough-going analytical and historical work. We are reminded of Marx's youthful aphorism, in response to the Young Hegelians' idea that 'criticism' could transform the world: 'The weapon of criticism must be replaced by the criticism of weapons!' How then did Marx 'criticize' capitalist society? Not simply by exploding the internal contradictions of Political Economy, but by showing how the struggle of the proletariat 'criticized' capitalism historically, by overthrowing it. (Marx refers, of course, to the nature of the proletariat as a class, and not in the first place to its conscious reactions: 'It does not matter what this or that proletarian, or even the whole proletariat, visualizes as the aim. Its aim and its historical action are prescribed irrefutably by its own life situation, as by the whole organization of contemporary bourgeois society'. *The Holy Family*.) Insofar as *Capital* grasped and presented scientifically *this* 'criticism', and demonstrated it to be the key to the whole mode of production and its development, Marx was satisfied with his work. Volume I of *Capital* is the general theoretical demonstration of the basic categories of capitalist economy from this standpoint. Both Volumes II and III were to move from this abstract presentation of the basic categories (with historical illustration for wage-labour and capital) to the world of everyday real appearances in which capitalist society functioned and through which the forces for its political overthrow were fashioned in conflict. Thus, in Volume III, the characteristic illusions of capitalist society are demonstrated in their origin and development, and finally Marx comes to the chapter 'Classes' in which, as one of his letters promised, he will deal with 'the class struggle, in which the whole thing is smashed up'.

Marx constantly stressed that Political Economy's claim to science was that, while involving a very high level of abstraction, it was concerned with the adequate reflection of objective phenomena, and not with 'pure' logical categories: 'Although an abstraction, this [value] is an historical abstraction which could only be adopted on the basis of a particular economic development of society'. (Letter to Engels, April 2, 1858.)

By the time *Capital*, Vol. I, was written, Marx had completed his definition of this connection between the social relations, the general forms of consciousness to which they gave rise, and the 'scientific' analysis of those relations:

> Hence, when we bring the products of our labour into relation with each other as values, it is not because we see in these articles the material receptacles of homogeneous human labour. Quite the contrary: whenever, by an exchange, we equate as values our different products, by that very act we also equate, as human labour, the different kinds of human labour. We are not aware of this, nevertheless we do it . . .
>
> The character of having value, when once impressed upon products, obtains fixity only by reason of their acting and re-acting upon each other as quantities of value. These quantities vary continually, independently of the will, foresight and action of the producers. To them their own social action takes the form of the action of objects, which rule the producers instead of being ruled by them. It requires a fully developed production of commodities before, from accumulated experience alone, the scientific conviction springs up, that all the different kinds of private labour, which are carried on independently of each other and yet as spontaneously developed branches of the social division of labour, are continually being reduced to the quantitative proportions in which society requires them. (*Capital*, Vol. I, pp. 45-46.)

Where the production of commodities existed only in a weak form, then (as in the case of Aristotle) only brilliant and isolated precursors of the theory of value could arise. It was the later total domination of commodity-production and exchange value in capitalist society which made possible the classical economists' concept of value. Similarly Marx himself penetrated to the essential phenomena of *the transformation of labour-power into a commodity* and of *surplus-value as unpaid labour* on the basis of the development of the working class and its struggle. Scientific work consisted in re-working all the categories and concepts from these basic discoveries. Marx always derided the 'vulgar economists' of his own day when they held up the 'contradictory' phenomena of everyday life and contrasted them to the basic concepts of value, etc. These 'vulgar economists' did not have the historical justification of their 'classical' predecessors for a static view of capitalist society and its antagonisms. By now there predominated the class egoism of the bourgeoisie and its fear of the proletariat, and the 'inner connection' of everyday economic facts could not be seen without a complete change of class outlook: 'When the inner connection is grasped all theoretical belief in the permanent necessity of existing conditions breaks down before their practical collapse'. (Letter to Kugelmann, July 11, 1868).

In the term 'practical collapse' Marx returns to his point in the 'preface' to Volume I: to grasp the inner connections now means to grasp the significance and necessity of the forces which produce the collapse or overthrow of capitalist economy — and thereby the refutation of the economic categories which reflected it as something fixed, permanent, 'natural'. This was the outcome of Marx's 'critique' of political economy. Once the working class appears as an independent force, the task of science is to pose the problem of the *historical fate* of capitalism.

In the years following the completion of Volume I, Marx continued to lay great emphasis on this epistemological or 'philosophical' aspect of his own work, time and again insisting on the nature of scientific categories as consciously reproducing the real developments in nature and society, and from this vantage-point grasping the essence of all intellectual and ideological development. Commenting on the work of the German historian Maurer, he wrote to Engels:

> But what would old Hegel say in the next world if he heard that the general (*Algemeine*) in German and Norse means nothing but the common land (*Gemeinland*), and the *particular, Sundre, Besondere,* nothing but the separate property divided off from the common land? Here are the logical categories coming damn well out of 'our intercourse' after all. (March 25, 1868).

And later in the same year, referring specifically to economic categories:

> While Messrs. the Economists treat the question whether ground rent is payment for natural differences in the land, or merely interest on the capital invested in the land, as a pure conflict of dogmas, we have here (in Irish history) an actual life or death struggle between farmer and landlord on the question *of how far* the rent *should also* include, *in addition to* payment for the difference in the land, interest on the capital invested in it — not only by the landlord, but by the tenant. It is only by substituting for conflicting dogmas the conflicting facts and real contradictions which form their hidden background that we can transform political economy into a positive science.

'Capital' and historical materialism

It is evident that *Capital* is very much a continuation of and not a departure from the years of work which the young Marx had devoted to the materialist foundations of his method, arrived at through the critique of Hegelian philosophy. But Marx had not simply accepted materialism in the old philosophical sense: his *historical* materialism sees man, socially producing, as the subject of the historical process, not in the sense that history is a manifestation of the will of man, but in the sense that he produces his own world. In so far as the necessity of this historical self-production is not understood it appears 'blind' and conflicts with men's wills. Philosophy had understood this but had taken *understanding* of the necessity as equivalent to freedom. Marx, on the other hand, held that the real subject of history, man himself in his social production relations, could now become free by a revolutionary re-shaping of those relations which would give him overall and planned control over all the accumulated productive forces. For this, the existing ownership system, in which the productive forces were transformed into capital, must be overthrown. This was a historical imperative of which man must become conscious: the contradiction between socially organized production and private ownership was a developing one, which threw the working class into conflict with the capitalist class. Day-to-day social production, organized planfully within the capitalist enterprise as part of the total production, which is unplanned, and the relations between the units of which is regulated unconsciously, is one level of the practice by which man constantly transforms the world. At a higher level, the conflict *between* the productive forces which more and more control nature and the capitalist production relations which inhibit them, requires a conscious understanding of the social system in its contradictory totality; an understanding which can be developed only in contradictory unity with the actual experience and struggle of that force which overthrows capitalism, the working class.

The subject-matter of classical political economy was the production and distribution of the wealth of capitalist society, conceived as a natural and timeless system. The subject-matter of 'vulgar economics' (i.e. of bourgeois economics after Ricardo) is the appearances of relations between products and between men as owners of those products. The subject-matter of Marx's *Capital* is 'to lay bare the economic law of motion of modern society'. In so doing, Marx presents the standpoint of 'socialized humanity' as against that of 'the isolated individual in civil society': humanity stands on the brink of social unity, abundance and control of its own destiny, because of the conquests of the productive forces, the growth of science, and the universalization of human needs, brought to a head by the necessity of capital to 'constantly revolutionize the means of production'; the proletariat, alienated completely from the means of production, is compelled in struggle to realize its historical interests as a class by carrying humanity forward from capitalism; the proletariat is potentially 'socialized humanity'; to realize its potential it must break the established forms of society, state and ideology.

Capital analyses this contradictory process at the 'basic' level of relations of production. It is the most highly elaborated test of Marx's historical materialism. This does not mean that it is a complete analysis of capitalist society. The ideological and political forms of that society would have to be specifically examined on a basis just as detailed as Marx's work on the social relations of production. But Marx's *Capital* is the indispensable basis for this further work. Not only does it show the specific unity and contradictions of the capitalist mode of production in all its economic manifestations, it also shows how the most general assumptions and ways of conceiving social relations are produced by the process of capitalist production and distribution. For historical materialism it is not sufficient to treat 'ideology' as merely the rationalization of some easily grasped 'class interests'. But it is essential to grasp that in *Capital*, the study of the economic basis of capitalist society as a historical whole, Marx deals at the same time with the most general categories of social consciousness engendered by capitalism.

Characteristically, Marx's presentation shows these ideological forms in conflict and contradiction with the material reality to which his own method has penetrated, from the analysis of the commodity and its mystifications (fetishism), through money as the highest form of this fetishism, to the unfinished analysis in Volume III of the illusions about the source of profit, rent and wages, around which a whole inversion of the relation between subject and object is constructed. *Capital* is thus itself a deliberately devised weapon for the dissolution of the capitalist class's ideological defences. To break these ideological shackles (in this case the assumption of permanence and 'naturalness' of capitalism) and the institutional forms associated with them is, in Marx's historical materialism, a necessary creative act in man's progress from one epoch to another. In this sense, the purpose of *Capital,* as of all Marx's writings, is to provide the consciousness which will assist man to free himself from the outmoded and oppressive social forms grown up on the basis of his past productive achievements. This 'revolutionary practice' is the real freedom which Marx opposes to the illusory freedom of the citizen under capitalism. By establishing consciously its true relationship with the productive forces (of which it is itself the principal one), the proletariat makes the 'leap to freedom'. *Capital* is the dramatic life-history of these productive forces and of this proletariat in struggle against capitalist production relations. The labour process in its capitalist form both reproduces capitalist society every day and yet by that same reproduction necessitates revolutionary change. Capitalist social relations are shown by Marx to be *necessary* forms for the development of the productive forces which *become* barriers to further development.

The basic relations of capitalism

Marx's *Capital* sets out to deal with '*the relations between capital and labour, the axis on which our entire present system of society turns*'. (Engels *On Capital*). (My emphasis — C.S.). It is this unified and organic view which has been the target of all sociological criticisms of Marxism. It clearly involves a thoroughly radical critique and rejection of the self-sufficiency of every part of social life and of the 'sociologies' which study them; it insists on the reference of all social phenomena to their true relation with this 'axis', the relation between capital and labour and its changes.

All labour, in capitalist society, is wage-labour. Labour-power is bought and sold as a commodity, like every other commodity. Not only labour-power, but also all implements of production and raw materials of production, in capitalist society, are transformed into capital. Before the production of human social life can take place for one second, capital must be differentiated into *constant capital*, which is invested in the raw materials and instruments of production, and variable capital, invested in labour-power, i.e. paid in wages. Between the value of labour-power and the value created by labour, which manifests itself only in the product, i.e. in the *consumption* of labour-power by the capitalist who has bought it, there is a difference. This difference or unpaid labour is *surplus-value,* and is the source of all the rent, interest and profit in capitalist society; the appropriation of this surplus-value is the mode of exploitation of capitalism. Only labour produces value: the other elements entering into the product merely have their original value *preserved* in the product.

The capitalist system of production carries to its furthest extreme the separation of the labourer from the means of production. In the historical sections of *Capital,* Marx describes the evolution of these conditions, the 'freeing' of the labourer from the soil or from his workshop, and the accumulation of all wealth by the capitalists. Here is the source of the 'alienation' about which so much has been written in recent years. When the capitalist buys labour-power, he is interested in it solely for the reproduction of the value of his capital, augmented by surplus value. The 'use-values' produced are of no interest as such. The 'concrete' or particular type of labour involved is of no interest as such. It is the general, abstract, value-producing character of the labour, common to *all* labour, which is of interest. All qualitative relationships are rendered irrelevant, as contrasted with previous modes of production.

> If we consider the process of production from the point of view of the simple labour-process, the labourer stands in relation to the means of production, not in their quality as capital, but as the mere means and material of his own intelligent productive activity . . . But it is different as soon as we deal with the process of production from the point of view of the process of creation of surplus-value. The means of production are at once changed into means for the absorption of the labour of others. It is now no longer the labourer that employs the means of production, but the means of production that employ the labourer. Instead of being consumed by him as material elements of his productive activity, they consume him as the ferment necessary to their own life-process, and the life-process of capital consists only in its movement as value constantly expanding, constantly multiplying itself. Furnaces and workshops that stand idle by night, and absorb no living labour, are 'a mere loss' to the capitalist. Hence, furnaces and workshops constitute lawful claims upon the night-labour of the work-people. The simple transformation of money into the material factors of the process of production, into means of production, transforms the latter into a title and a right to the labour and surplus-labour of others . . . (and) this complete inversion of the relation between dead and living labour, between value and the force that creates value, mirrors itself in the consciousness of capitalists. (*Capital*, Volume I, pp. 297-298).

For an understanding of the diametrically opposed starting-points and subject-matter of Marxism on the one hand and sociology on the other, there could be no clearer text than the above quotation. From it flows the Marxian analysis of fetishism and ideology under capitalism, as well as the basic course of the class struggle which will eventually close the capitalist chapter of history. At the same time it indicates the historical limits of capitalism in the past: the creation of its historical preconditions, i.e. wage-labour freed from the land and instruments of production, and accumulated capital free to appropriate the latter. Where sociologists will devote their attention, say, to roles and statuses as functions of the division of labour in an 'industrial' society, Marx is interested first and foremost in the social relations of production. These are *not* produced by the needs of 'industry' as such, but by the *capitalist* mode of production. Instead of starting, say, with the need for technical, supervisory, clerical and manual workpeople, Marx begins with the social relations: no labour can be applied to means of production unless and until the labourer first *sells* his labour-power to the owner of the means of production. *All production passes through this set of relations*. To Marxists, the phenomenon of daily authority relations between supervisors and workmen, for example, is of minor importance: from the point of view of the capitalist system, it is the fact that man is subjected to the *unconscious* authority of the market and the laws of accumulation of capital that predominates. To indicate the implications of such a distinction: it is at this level of the system that the question of conflict with 'authority' must be tackled and resolved, and not, as sociology supposes, at the level of individual reactions to the imposition of the will of others in superior positions; on the one hand, questions of class-consciousness at the level of the system and its historical destiny, and on the other, questions of individual or 'group' response to status differences.

By starting with these 'social relations' in general (the approach of 'sociology'), Marx arrives at distinctions which are in sharp contrast to the assumptions of sociology. For example, his treatment of division of labour and authority, touched upon above, is strictly tied to his concepts of the capitalist mode of production, and examples from other social orders are considered only by contrast with these specifically capitalist relations. Man in capitalist society is subject to the domination of the laws of the market as an outside force whose caprices are beyond his conscious control. The proportions between different branches of industry, the allocation of society's total labour time into these different branches, is regulated by the unconscious laws of the market. At the same time, within the given enterprise, capital requires authority just as absolute but of a totally different kind: the undisputed will of the capitalist (or his agent) to co-ordinate all the elements of production. '. . . anarchy in the social division of labour and despotism in that of the workshop are mutual conditions the one of the other . . .' (Ibid, p. 350.)

This is in stark contrast with previous modes of production, in which division of labour *within* the unit of production is non-existent, and yet social life outside it is more strictly regulated and controlled. In all these earlier forms, 'On the whole, the labourer and his means of production remained closely united, like the snail with its shell, and thus there was wanting the principal basis of manufacture, the separation of the labourer from his means of production, and the conversion of those means into capital.' (Ibid, p. 353)

Before dealing with the treatment of forms of social consciousness in *Capital*, we quote Marx himself on the specific contribution which he considered he had made to the understanding of capitalist production relations. This must replace, in the space here available, any extended account of the development of the argument in Marx's main work. Writing to Engels, Marx referred to 'the three fundamentally new elements' of *Capital:*

> (1) That in contrast to *all* former systems of political economy, which *begin* by taking the particular fragments of surplus value with their fixed forms of rent, profit, and interest as already given, I first deal with the general form of surplus value, in which all these elements are still undifferentiated — in solution as it were.
>
> (2) That, without exception, the economists have missed the simple point that if the commodity has a double character — use value and exchange value — then the labour represented in the commodity must also have a double character, while the mere bald analysis of labour, as in Smith, Ricardo, etc., is bound to come up everywhere against the inexplicable. This is, in fact, the whole secret of the critical conception.
>
> (3) That for the first time wages are shown as the *irrational form* in which a hidden relation appears, and this is exactly represented in the two forms of wage payment — time wages and piece wages. (It was a help to me that similar formulae are often found in higher mathematics.) (Marx, letter to Engels, 8 January 1868.)

Those 'fundamentally new elements' are precisely those aspects of the capitalist economic order which are perceived only by penetrating beneath the appearance of free exchange of commodities (including labour, in the old conception) in everyday capitalist intercourse. These new categories reflect the *single* force of creation of all new value (including, of course, surplus value) which resides in the proletariat. This proletariat can grasp its own essence and its historical role only by grasping the *system* theoretically in the way that Marx does. As we shall see later (Chapter V), the division of society into classes, and their mutual interrelations, must be seen in terms of this production and reproduction of the total value, and not in terms of their external characteristics.

Capitalism and ideology

> It is only through the habit of everyday life that we come to think it perfectly plain and common-place that a social relation of production should take on the form of a thing, so that the relation of persons in their work appears in the form of a mutual relation between things, and between things and persons. (Marx, *Contribution to the Critique of Political Economy*, 1859.)

Whereas for Marx the relations of production constitute the basic economic structure of society, the 'form' taken by those relations (in capitalism, the 'form of a thing') gives us the general characteristics of the institutions and ideology of the society in question. It will therefore be useful to indicate the social and ideological forms first analysed in *Capital*.

When Marx begins his book with 'commodities' he is doing this in order to find that point at which it is possible to penetrate from the surface to the essential production relations. Commodities exchange against each other in ways which seem to flow from their actual properties as things, and every one of them can be equated with definite proportions of every other and with the universal equivalent, money. When Marx begins *Capital*, however, with the statement that '... The wealth of these societies in which the capitalist mode of production prevails, presents itself as "an immense accumulation of commodities", its unit being a single commodity. Our analysis must therefore begin with the analysis of a commodity', it should not be forgotten that in the earlier essay, *Contribution to the Critique of Political Economy* (1859) these words are preceded by the phrase, 'At first sight . . .'. Marx does not dismiss this appearance as simple delusion: it is the *actual*, living, everyday form in which man's products *are* exchanged. Men do confront the product of their creative social efforts *only* as commodities, only through exchange: the total wealth 'presents itself' as a vast accumulation of commodities. In capitalist society *no* mutual relations between the producers take shape except by going through this form of relationship, which expresses and at the same time obscures the relation between the different parts of the total social labour. It is clear that for Marx therefore, exploitation can be abolished only by abolishing the property relation between wage-labour and capital, a 'social relation of production' which enables the capitalists to appropriate the surplus product, the difference between the value of labour power and the value produced by labour.

That each commodity should have a *use-value* is of course essential to its existence. But this characteristic of every product, together with its corollary, the variety of concretely different types of labour producing different commodities, is common to all human societies, and thus can tell us nothing about the specific social relations of the capitalist system. The use-value of a product remains in principle the same regardless of whether it is immediately consumed, bartered or sold as a commodity. The proportions in which use-values are exchanged are decided by something external to the specific properties of use-values or of each form of concrete labour which produces them. Commodities exchange in strict equivalence with one another in a way which negates their different particular characteristics. The common substance which permits this exchangeability is the general or 'abstract' labour embodied in them; and in this abstract form, producing exchange-value, labour is measured by time. 'As exchange values, all commodities are but definite measures of *congealed labour-time*.' *Capital* must therefore go beneath what was seen 'at first sight' to the forms in which this labour is brought into production.

In other forms of society, the men performing different types of concrete labour are not brought into mutual relation through the relations between things (products), as portions of the total labour of society divided according to the socially necessary labour-time involved in their production, as under capitalism. On the contrary, production in earlier societies is a direct and transparent expression of the social organism. In a patriarchal peasant economy production is the direct expression of 'the family organization with its natural division of labour'. In primitive societies, 'individual labour appears as the direct function of a member of the social organism.' In feudal society, 'because personal dependence forms the groundwork of society', labour and exploitation take the direct form of services and payment in kind. In a socialist 'community of free individuals' the labour-power of individuals would be 'consciously applied as the combined labour-power of the community'.

Contrast this with capitalist society: the individual worker or capitalist begins *only* from his individual needs; the social character of his labour *becomes* apparent and achieves definite form in relation to its social equivalents, establishes its relations with them, *only* afterwards, through the act of exchange, through realizing itself as universal, abstract labour. The *value-form* is therefore a key concept, expressing the typical and historically necessary form by which individual acts and actors are brought into a social relationship. In the non-scientific consciousness, however, this *way in which* the social relations are concretized (the value-form) is mistaken for the social relations themselves. The mutual relations between producers are transposed into the value-relation between their products. Men are dominated by these relations between things. The universal exchange achieved by capitalism makes mankind the single subject and creator of all the means of life, but these means take on an 'objective' form which inverts the real relation. Man's labour is called upon or not called upon, used or not used, rewarded or not rewarded, according to the requirements of these products and the laws of their exchange, and, at a higher level, their augmentation in the form of capital. Just as all labour becomes wage-labour, so do all products of past labour not immediately consumed become capital, and enter the production process only in order to make capital grow. *'Dead labour' dominates over 'living labour'*.

Christianity, said Marx, was admirably suited to commodity production and particularly, in its Protestant forms, to capitalism, because of its 'cultus of abstract man', reflecting the irrelevance of qualitative differences in labour in these social relations. Primitive religions, on the other hand, propounded a doctrine of direct relations between men, their immediate natural environment, and the limited historical and cultural horizons of isolated communities. Communism, the community of free individuals, will lay the basis for abolition of all religion, because there 'the practical relations of everyday life offer to man none but perfectly intelligible and reasonable relations with his fellow-men and to nature'. (*Capital*, Volume I, p. 51). Here Marx expands the thoughts first put down in his *Critique of*

Hegel's Philosophy of Right, in which the famous 'religion is the opium of the people' occurs.

It should be added here that the everyday relations between products or between men under capitalist production are produced through a more complex development than that of simple commodity production. The discrepancy between 'value' and 'price' arises not only from the price mechanism and the fluctuations of supply and demand but from another and more basic fact.

> The whole difficulty arises from the fact that commodities are not exchanged simply as *commodities*, but as *products of capitals*, which claim participation in the total amount of surplus-value, proportional to their magnitude, or equal if they are of equal magnitude. (Ibid, Volume III, p. 200.)

Money has a very important role in the mystification of capitalist relations (a real or 'prosaic' mystification, as Marx pointed out, not a mystery of the mind). It was a historical prerequisite in highly developed form for the process of primitive capital accumulation to take place. It is the form taken by capital itself, and does not simply function as measure of value, universal equivalent, and means of exchange. It is money which unites, in concrete form, the opposites in the commodity form. Every commodity is not only priced, and thereby related to every other commodity, but is itself a general equivalent for every other commodity, despite its appeal as use-value to only a very limited number of consumers. With money, '... we find in one commodity the solution of the contradiction which is inherent in commodity as such, viz., of being at one and the same time a particular use-value and a universal equivalent, and, therefore, a use-value for everybody or universal use-value'. Money is not just a theoretical equivalent, but actually endows its possessor with the power to command *all* use-values, it is a 'universal use-value'.

Men in capitalist society (and in highly developed commodity production) find money already established as the universal equivalent. It is natural that they tend to see gold, silver and banknotes as possessing the intrinsic ability to command definite proportions of every other commodity in the world (including the whole of past culture and achievement, as in great paintings). Gold and silver, says Marx, are accepted as coming out of the earth with universal values stamped all over them, 'the direct incarnation of all human labour'.

Money in its various roles is an actual solvent and creator of social relations. To the members of society, this situation appears to flow from the power of money *as such*. These specific illusions in all their forms, are a necessary object for the study of all capitalism's social and ideological forms. It is not just a question of false consciousness of the economy, consisting of the inversion of subject and object and the habit of thought which sees separate 'facts' or objects as coming ready-made with their own 'value' to the 'market' of interaction with the rest of the world. These are characteristic forms throughout the ideological superstructure. They were to a certain extent present in other social systems in which commodity production existed, but they are taken to an extreme degree by capitalism and its 'free', atomised individuals, just as capitalism takes to the extreme the process of alienation and the production of 'wealth' for its own sake. Its tendency is to dissolve *all* local and particular, communal, directly personal relationships, to sever all organic and traditional ties, to substitute the 'cash nexus' as Carlyle and the traditionalists called it, for these relationships. What was a *tendency* towards the abstract contemplation of isolated facts in previous epochs now develops freely, without any restrictions in the social basis of men's experience and ideas. This transformation in the ideological sphere does not take place automatically, but through struggle against the survivals of earlier forms of thought and through the ruling classes or the persistence of archaic social forms. The conformity of ideology to economy takes place only unconsciously, not in a planned way, and by a series of adjustments, the significance of which may vary greatly in different spheres of ideology. But we find the tendency towards individualism and abstractness predominates in religion, philosophy, political theory and creative literature under capitalism.

To sustain this argument would require not simply a reference to parallels at the economic and ideological levels, but a detailed examination of the contradictory processes through which changes have taken place, in a struggle of real social forces and not by 'adaptation' to the economic basis. Marx carried out such an analysis for the political ideologies of 19th century Europe and for political economy, and a number of Marxists have carried the analysis into other fields. We confine ourselves only to some aspects of Marx's elaboration of the characteristic ideological products of the capitalist system in *Capital* itself.

By 'commodity fetishism' Marx means then 'the objective appearance of the social characteristics of labour'. In other words, men's own mutual relations as social producers appear to them in the form of set characteristics of material objects, the products of their labour. That the *proportions of the total labour-time* expended on particular products should appear to men *only* in the form and through the measure of the *magnitude of the exchange-value of material objects* indicates with certainty, says Marx, a mode of production in which 'the process of production has the mastery over man, instead of being controlled by him'.

This conclusion, emphasising as it does the actual oppression of the producers by the system of capitalist production, and not just the distortion of their consciousness, indicates one of the essential aspects in which Marxism is differentiated from sociology. Marx does not see labour as a process which goes on in some 'independent' fashion determined directly by the level of productive technique and its demands on the division of labour, with 'social relations' built on top of this foundation. For him, the social relations are not just forms of interaction, or even of appropriation and distribution, but are built into the labour-process itself, in this case by all labour being first and foremost value-creating labour, labour for capital's purposes (and of course by means of production entering the process *only* as capital). In the distinction between *labour-power* 'owned' by the propertyless worker and sold to the capitalist, and *labour* entirely controlled and its product entirely appropriated by the capitalist, man the producer is brutally separated from the man who fulfils himself (cf. P. Naville, *De l'Aliénation à la Jouissance*, Paris 1957). In *Capital* Marx makes precise and objective the insights of his earlier works on 'alienation', which is now posed not philosophically and morally but by a rigorous analysis of the actual process by which man is reduced to an owner of mere labour-power and then, through the perfectly legal 'alienation' of this commodity, exploited through capital being able to appropriate the difference between the value of labour-power and the value produced by labour.

This 'domination of dead labour (capital) over living labour' was formulated by Marx in the *Communist Manifesto* (written 1847, published 1848) in a general way, which indicates its significance for ideology as a whole in capitalist society: 'In bourgeois society capital is independent and has individuality, while the living person is dependent and has no individuality.' In Volume I of *Capital* he is more specific:

> The life process of capital consists only in its movement as value constantly expanding, constantly multiplying itself . . .

> The simple transformation of money into the material factors of the process of production, into means of production, transforms the latter into a title and a right to the labour and surplus-labour of others . . . This sophistication, peculiar to and characteristic of capitalist production, this complete inversion of the relation between dead and living labour, between value and the power that creates value, mirrors itself in the consciousness of the capitalist. (*Capital*, Volume I, pp. 297-298.)

Later, in Volume III, Marx takes the various forms of capital, and shows how the fetishism proliferates:

> Now, the concept of capital as a fetish reaches its height in interest-bearing capital, being a conception which attributes to the accumulated product of labour, and at that in the fixed form of money, the inherent secret power, as an automaton, of creating surplus-value in geometrical progression, so that the accumulated product of labour, as the *Economist* thinks, has long discounted all the wealth of the world for all time as belonging to it and rightfully coming to it. The product of past labour, the past labour itself, is here pregnant in itself with a portion of present or future surplus-value. We know, however, that in reality the preservation, and to that extent also the reproduction of the value of products of past labour is *only* the result of their contact with living labour; and secondly, that the domination of the products of past labour over living surplus-labour lasts only as long as the relation of capital, which rests on those particular social relations in which past labour independently and overwhelmingly dominates over living labour. (*Capital*, Volume III, pp. 390-391.)

In passing, it should be noted that it is in this general view of the capitalist system as domination of dead (past) labour over the living, that all Marx's notes in Volume III about the separation of ownership and control, the credit system and the joint-stock company, must be understood.

Dahrendorf (*Class and Class Conflict in Industrial Society*) has characterized these writings as a confused recognition by Marx of the incorrectness of his view of the antagonistic basic property relations of capitalism. However, Marx is undoubtedly presenting the contradiction of the capitalist system in what he considers to be a sharpening of this antagonism. From the large number of possible illustrations, the following are typical:

> . . . hence, instead of overcoming the antithesis between the character of wealth as social and as private wealth, the stock companies merely develop it in a new form. (p. 431)

> With the development of social production the means of production cease

to be means of private production, and can thereafter be only means of production in the hands of associated producers, i.e., the latter's social property, much as they are their social products. However, this expropriation appears within the capitalist system in a contradictory form, as appropriation of social property by a few; and credit lends the latter more and more the aspect of pure adventures . . . (p. 430)

This is a modest distance from Dahrendorf's summary of Marx's view of the joint-stock company as 'half-way to Communism'. But this 'misunderstanding' arises from a deeper and wider divergence between Marxism and bourgeois sociology. Dahrendorf, like Parsons and other bourgeois sociologists, is starting from the 'differentiation' of the capitalist nineteenth-century 'role', especially the separation of ownership and control (management), and its consequences for power and authority relations. Marx's concern is with the social structure arising from the interaction between *classes* (wage-labour and capital) first at the economic level (production) and then politically. The nature of the social integration which takes place under capitalism is through and consequent upon the act of exchange of commodities. The movement of the whole is independent of the will of the participants in the interaction. In the different spheres of social activity in which individuals are engaged, they act consciously with definite orientations and have the illusion of freedom in choice of ends and means. There is no direct 'determination' of their orientation in any particular sphere by 'economics'. Thus when a sociology of roles and orientations is used to explain a series of actions in a given situation, it will provide a more or less accurate guide to the actions of the individuals concerned. But it can say nothing about the implications of these for the social system, just as it can say nothing about how the conditions of existence of this particular set of orientations came into being, and what the relationship is between these basic conditions and the particular set of orientations under investigation: the relations and limits of the changes in each of them can be approached only with a theory and method whose categories derive from the social whole, from its structure, its internal contradictions. All those in the workers' movement who resort to explanation in terms of motives should take warning from the fact that bourgeois sociology has resorted to precisely this *idealist* method (values, orientations, etc.) in the attempt to refute Marxism.

Here we return to Marx's stress on social relations of production. The whole society can subsist from day to day only through the constant repetition of this exploitative relationship to which hundreds of millions are subjected in every country in the world. The very metabolism of capitalist society takes its essential form from this exchange and conflict between classes. It is not as if 'production' takes place according only to some technical necessity, and then a series of social conflicts and relationships grows up in the course of a social life built on the foundation of industry. Men perceive their social relations, and conceptualise other men and their characteristics, material objects and their characteristics, only in the course of social experience structured by those fundamental relations. The 'roles' which form the basic category of bourgeois sociology are not neutral units out of which different social structures might be built, but are the worked-out consequences of this subordination of man together with his capacities and his material and intellectual products. Role-sociology accepts the fragmented and alien capacities of capitalist society's men as 'objective' data; a Marxist 'sociology' would set itself the task of consistently and critically explaining these roles from the starting point of the contradiction in the capitalist economic foundation: man's needs are universalised, 'socialised' to the highest degree; yet men confront each other not only as individuals entering the production process purely to enable them to consume or to augment capital, but also with each man divided against himself, a part of him being demanded, with the requisite 'economy', for each activity into which he enters, because their activities have a false separateness and men seek human satisfaction within one or more of these alienated spheres, the true character of which could only be grasped and humanly enjoyed through its creative reintegration with the social whole; to achieve that, consciousness must be directed to the mobilization of the social force which can remove the source of alienation.

Marx gave only a preliminary specific indication of this work but, as we have pointed out, his own exposition in *Capital* is its indispensable foundation. He writes there:

> It is not the place, here, to go on to show how division of labour seizes upon not only the economical, but every other sphere of society, and everywhere lays the foundation of that all-engrossing system of specialising and sorting men, that development in a man of one single faculty at the expense of all other faculties, which caused A. Ferguson, the master of Adam Smith, to exclaim: 'We make a nation of helots, and have no free citizens'. (*Capital*, Volume I, p. 347.)

This tendency in the division of labour is not only taken to its extreme in capitalist industry, but is combined with a social division of labour through the commodity and exploitation relations we have outlined, with their subordination of every capacity to profit, and with the universal inversion of the relation between subject and object. Out of the situation created by this arise the illusions of the free 'individual' confronting millions of 'choices'.* 'Sociology' proceeds by quantifying and passing judgment upon these results and symptoms, never penetrating to their source.

This sociological method leads not only to superficiality of analysis but to an apologia for the existing capitalist class structure. The incomes of the capitalist, the landlord and the worker appear to be 'rewards' for the participation in production of capital (invested in machines, raw materials, etc), land, and labour, and the values accruing to each appear to arise independently out of each of these sources. Marx showed in *Capital* that the *historical* class position of capitalists, of propertyless wage-labourers and of landed proprietors produced a situation where 'capital attracts to the capitalist, in the form of profit, a portion of the surplus value extracted by him from labour, that monopoly in land attracts for the landlord another portion in the form of rent; and that labour grants the labourer the remaining portion of value in the form of wages'. (Ibid, Volume III, p. 807.) *All* these are separate portions of the same value created by labour, but under capitalism 'these productive powers and the social interrelation of labour in the direct labour-process seem transferred from labour to capital. Capital thus becomes a very mystic being since all of labour's social productive forces appear to be due to capital, rather than labour as such, and seem to issue from the womb of capital itself'. (Ibid, p. 806.)

The daily round of business confirms these illusions millions of times. Because the law of value asserts itself only through chance variations in price on the market, affording opportunities to the businessman to exercise his individual ingenuity, and often increase his rate of profit as against competitors, he entertains the belief that the source of his profit is his own ability as the personification of his

---

* Marx notes that at another level of social interaction, outside the sphere of production, certain human qualities are transformed in character. 'The price-form . . . may conceal a qualitative inconsistency, so much so, that, although money is nothing but the value-form of commodities, price ceases altogether to express value. Objects that in themselves are not commodities, such as conscience, honour, etc., are capable of thus acquiring, through their price, the form of commodities.' (*Capital*, Vol. 1, p. 75.)

capital. The relation between the property relations, the production process, and the process of circulation, in the formation of these forms of consciousness must be noted:

> The way in which surplus-value is transformed into the form of profit by way of the rate of profit is, however, a further development of the inversion of subject and object that takes place already in the process of production. In the latter, we have seen, the subjective productive forces of labour appear as productive forces of capital. On the one hand, the value or the past labour, which dominates living labour, is incarnated in the capitalist. On the other hand, the labourer appears as bare material labour-power, as a commodity. Even in the simple relations of production this inverted relationship necessarily produces certain correspondingly inverted conceptions, a transposed consciousness which is further developed by the metamorphoses and modifications of actual circulation process. (Ibid, p. 45.)

The 'sphere of circulation' is:

> The sphere of competition, which, considered in each individual case, is dominated by chance; where, then, the inner law, which prevails in these accidents and regulates them, is only visible when these accidents are grasped together in large numbers, where it remains, therefore, invisible and unintelligible to the individual agents in production. But furthermore: the actual process of production, as a unity of the direct production process and the circulation process, gives rise to new formations, in which the vein of internal connections is increasingly lost, the production relations are rendered independent of one another, and the component values become ossified into forms independent of one another. (Ibid, p. 807.)

The whole chapter, 'The Trinity Formula' (Chapter XLVIII, *Capital*, Volume III) is a preliminary elaboration of the way in which these ideological distortions take place. In supposing that capital gives rise to profit, land to rent, and labour to wages, the capitalist ideologists arrive at 'the complete mystification of the capitalist mode of production, the direct coalescence of the material production relations with their industrial and social determination. It is an enchanted, perverted, topsy-turvy world, in which Monsieur le Capital and Madame la Terre do their ghost-walking as social characters and at the same time as mere things.' (Ibid p. 809.)

Classical political economy 'destroyed this false appearance and illusion' but remained captured within the capitalist form of society, 'as cannot be otherwise from the bourgeois standpoint and thus they all fall more or less into inconsistencies, half truths and unresolved contradictions'. The 'vulgar economists', who succeeded them, says

Marx, cannot however go beyond the vulgar conceptions of the everyday participants in capitalist economy, simply 'arranging them in a certain rational order'. The 'Trinity Formula' at which they arrive 'simultaneously corresponds to the interests of the ruling classes by proclaiming the physical necessity and eternal justification of their sources of revenue and elevating them to a dogma'. (Ibid, p. 810.)

A Marxist critique of sociology would demonstrate the latter's continuation of the traditions of 'vulgar economy' into the general category of 'social' and not only economic relations.

Long before writing his major work, which he intended to be the basis for an analysis of all the social and political institutions of capitalism, Marx had bitingly anticipated such a critique in what reads like an epitaph on 'functionalist' sociology before its birth:

> A philosopher produces ideas, a poet verses, a parson sermons, a professor text-books, etc. A criminal produces crime. But if the relationship between this latter branch of production and the whole productive activity of society is examined a little more closely one is forced to abandon a number of prejudices. The criminal produces not only crime but also the criminal law; he produces the professor who delivers lectures on this criminal law, and even the inevitable text-book in which the professor presents his lectures as a commodity for sale in the market. There results an increase in material wealth, quite apart from the pleasure which . . . the author himself derives from the manuscript of this text-book.
>
> Further, the criminal produces the whole apparatus of the police and criminal justice, detectives, judges, executioners, juries, etc., and all these different professions, which constitute so many categories of the social division of labour, develop diverse abilities of the human spirit, create new needs and new ways of satisfying them. Torture itself has provided occasions for the most ingenious mechanical inventions, employing a host of honest workers in the production of these instruments.
>
> The criminal produces an impression now moral, now tragic, and renders a 'service' by arousing the moral and aesthetic sentiments of the public. He produces not only text-books on criminal law, the criminal law itself, and thus legislators, but also art, literature, novels and the tragic drama, Oedipus and Richard III, as well as Mullner's Schuld and Schiller's Räuber, testify. The criminal interrupts the monotony and security of bourgeois life. Thus he protects it from stagnation and brings forth that restless tension, that mobility of spirit without which the stimulus of competition would itself become blunted. He therefore gives a new impulse to the productive forces. Crime takes off the labour market a portion of the excess population, diminishes competition among workers, and to a certain extent stops wages from falling below the minimum, while

the war against crime absorbs another part of the same population. The criminal therefore appears as one of those natural 'equilibrating forces' which establish a just balance and open up a whole perspective of 'useful' occupations. The influence of the criminal upon the development of the productive forces can be shown in detail. Would the locksmith's trade have attained its present perfection if there had been no thieves? Would the manufacture of banknotes have arrived at its present excellence if there had been no counterfeiters? Would the microscope have entered ordinary commercial life (cf. Babbage) had there been no forgers? Is not the development of applied chemistry as much due to the adulteration of wares, and to the attempts to discover it, as to honest productive effort? Crime, by its ceaseless development of new means of attacking property calls into existence new measures of defence, and its productive effects are as great as those of strikes in stimulating the invention of machines.

Leaving the sphere of private crime, would there be a world market, would nations themselves exist, if there had not been national crimes? Is not the tree of evil also the tree of knowledge, since the time of Adam?

In his *Fable of the Bees* (1708) Mandeville already demonstrated the productivity of all the English occupations, and anticipated our argument. 'What we call Evil in this World, Moral as well as Natural, is the grand Principle that makes us sociable Creatures, the solid Basis, the Life and Support of all Trades and Employments without Exception That there we must look for the true Origin of all Arts and Sciences, and that the moment Evil ceases, the Society must be spoiled if not totally dissolved.'

Mandeville simply had the merit of being infinitely more audacious and more honest than these narrow-minded apologists for bourgeois society. (Marx. *Theories of Surplus Value*, cited in Bottomore and Rubel, op cit.)

The so-called 'social sciences' of modern bourgeois scholarship, especially sociology, are the continuation of these apologetics into the period of social revolution and the overthrow of capitalism. Marxism has developed in the intervening period, not as a 'dialogue' with, or 'criticism' of, these apologists, but as the conscious construction of a revolutionary party, developing its theory independently through the struggle for leadership in the working class, and *only from this standpoint* analysing bourgeois ideology in order to understand better capitalism's crisis and Marxism's own revolutionary tasks.

VII
Marxist theory and class consciousness

Marxism is not a 'sociology'. It only appears to be so, because, from the point of view of every other particular section of the intellectual division of labour — philosophy, economics, history, history of ideas, etc. — Marxism goes beyond their defined subject-matter, insisting that the real content of each of them is to be found in the contradictory totality of social economic relations from which flow the forms of activity and thought to which the separate disciplines address themselves. Political economy, for example, is 'negated' by Marxism, in the Hegelian sense. Marx's treatment of political economy takes to their limit the contradictory developments of classical political economy. To do this requires the explanation of political economy's concepts and their real content as the 'alienated' consciousness of the development of bourgeois society itself. Thus we find in the *Critique of Political Economy* and in *Capital* itself a negation of political economy, which is demonstrated as being an adequate reflection of the sphere of exchange values and their behaviour. But this sphere is shown to be the real world of appearances or illusions as necessarily created by a historically limited social order, capitalism.

Marx's rejection of bourgeois philosophy is a similar materialist critique. His analysis of political and historical thought and their material sources was the third element of the synthesis achieved by Marx.

Why then do we say that Marxism only *appears to be* a sociology? Because sociology originated and developed, not as the dialectical negation, the overcoming of the contradictions, of each of the alienated spheres of thought, but as their definition anew in relation to some supposedly more 'general' science of the 'the social as such' (Durkheim's *'le social en soi'* and 'social facts' constitute the acme of this approach). Comte, first to use the term 'sociology', invented the word in order to indicate: '... under one single heading that integral part of natural philosophy which concerns itself with the positive study of the totality of fundamental laws proper to social phenomena.'

Instead of the dynamic synthesis constituted by Marx's negation of the separated and alienated fields of philosophy, political economy and history (class struggle), we have the static and uncritical synthesis of Comte, to be followed by a century of sterile debate in sociology about 'metaphysics or empiricism', 'generalization or specialized monographs', 'system or action'. Instead of the consistent materialism made possible by Marx's historical or dialectical approach, we have the pseudo-scientific reliance on 'experience', which in Comte's case ended in the purest mysticism, since his 'spiritual' experience was granted just as much validity as any other. Bourgeois sociology in the 20th century is tied, philosophically and methodologically, to the pragmatism of the ruling class. Sociology continues to oscillate between idealism and mechanical materialism: 'social facts as things' on the one hand, freedom of the individual on the other; the classical dichotomy of bourgeois ideology. Instead of social analysis in terms of the contradictory development and struggle of opposites in each specific, historically limited, socio-economic formation, we have in sociology the search for general principles or sociological laws which transcend specific historical stages. Talcott Parsons' rejection of Marxism, on the grounds that it is a series of 'genetic' explanations, sums up this functionalist barrenness.

These aspects of the split in social theory between Marxism and sociology since the second quarter of the last century are of course inseparably linked with the fact that, as against Marx and Marxism's concern with *capitalist* society, Comte is the father (though he himself is only the bastard son of Saint-Simon in this and many other respects) of the sociologists' insistence that they are concerned with 'industrial' or 'modern' society. This is only a 'sociological' version of the political economists' recognition of the 'natural' character of the laws of capitalist economy, which they could not accept as only the laws of a definite and historically limited socio-economic formation. When Marx insisted on the 'social' dimension of all spheres of activity and thought, it was with a dual emphasis: first, to grasp each sphere as only one 'moment' of a contradictory social whole; second, to put an end to the alienation resulting from exploitation, to give a new life to each activity by making it the conscious activity of the associated producers in a classless society; for this, theory must unite with and develop in unity with the proletarian revolution. Sociology, by contrast, accepts and describes the alienation and even dignifies it by presenting it systematically as the 'differentiation and integration of roles' and the 'structuring of orientations'. A Marxist analysis of sociology would demonstrate in what way these supposedly 'general' social phenomena and mechanisms are but an ideological reflection of the surface of capitalist society itself.

The revolutionary political orientation of Marxist social theory, as contrasted with the professed 'value-freedom' of sociology, is fundamental to Marxism. And the perennial pleas for separating Marx's politics from his sociological 'insights' are as absurdly misplaced as the similar attempts to cleanse Marx's social theories of philosophy.

Marxism is then the dialectical negation of the highest developments in bourgeois thought, and through this of the reality from which that thought flows and of which it forms a necessary part. It is this conception which lies behind Lenin's famous dictum:

> The workers can acquire political consciousness *only from without*, i.e., only outside of the economic struggle, outside of the sphere of relations between workers and employers. The sphere from which alone it is possible to obtain this knowledge is the sphere of relationships between *all* classes and the state and the government — the sphere of the interrelations between all *classes*. (Lenin, *What is to be Done?*)

Here Lenin expresses politically (i.e. in conflict with political opponents who based themselves on the supposed 'spontaneous' development of socialist consciousness from the experience of the working class) the implications for working-class consciousness of the discoveries of Marx. Scientific thought (in the philosophy of Hegel) had arrived at the point where it must accept the conclusion that it could advance further only by grasping actively its real place in the struggle to end the conditions of its own alienated character; this was only possible, Marx said, by grasping the nature of the working class as the agent of the necessary revolutionary change. The working class itself, however, could arrive at the necessary consciousness and thereby the unity necessary for social revolution only by understanding the full historical implications of its role in production and its capacity for abolishing class society. Besides the conclusion that the economic structure is 'basic', and that the class struggle of the proletariat is an objective necessity creating the conditions for socialist revolution, there was necessary the whole theory of historical materialism, the understanding of social development as a unified process, with revolutionary consciousness seizing hold of the meaning of the contradictions at the base of society in order to overthrow it. This body of theory could not come from the working class but only 'from the outside, from bourgeois intellectuals'. From that point on, the development of Marxism takes definite forms in relation to the struggle of the working class, its internal political conflicts, strategy, tactics and organization, nationally and internationally. While Marx and Engels themselves made great contributions in this field, it has of course been most enriched in the twentieth century, above all by the work of Lenin and Trotsky.

Marx and Engels began their communist political careers with a series of thoroughgoing polemics against other schools of socialism (e.g., in *The Communist Manifesto*). Immediately after the 1848 revolutions they combated the impatience and what amounted to rejection of theory by those who wanted to continue an insurrectionist struggle in unfavourable conditions. They never ceased to participate in and advise the labour movement in every country with which they could establish contact. They insisted — for example, in correspondence with Russian and North American socialists — on a very close and detailed attention to the specific conditions of the history, economy and working-class movement of each particular country. But they always were vigilant against eclecticism and attempts to put aside the theoretical conquests they had made. Writing to Bebel and other leaders of the German Social-Democratic Party in 1879, Marx and Engels returned to a theme which had concerned them as long ago as 1848: the role of bourgeois intellectuals in the revolutionary movement. Then, in the *Manifesto*, they had written: '. . . a small section of the ruling class cuts itself adrift, and joins the revolutionary class . . . in particular, a portion of the bourgeois ideologists.'

Now, in 1879, they make a very different emphasis, and one which shows that Lenin was not inconsistent when he combined his insistence on the decisive importance of intellectuals in the development of revolutionary theory with an implacable struggle against every manifestation of revisionism and intellectual light-mindedness with theory. Marx and Engles go out of their way to warn Bebel and the party leaders that bourgeois and petty-bourgeois intellectuals joining the movement must show that they are willing to *learn* from the party its theory of scientific socialism in the first place. If this is not done, then they inevitably bring with them elements of the *now* decaying and disintegrating German bourgeois culture and philosophy. (In other words, what could be *gained* from bourgeois development before 1848 was the *opposite* of what flowed from it in 1789.)

Lenin stressed that the fight against revisionism (so called after the celebrated controversy in the German Social Democracy over Bernstein's criticisms of Marx in the 1890s) was a recurring and inevitable one. He explained that not only individual thinkers in the working class or the revolutionary Marxist party were affected by particular aspects of bourgeois ideology, but that the development of capitalism constantly modified the relations between the proletariat and the middle classes, the latter carrying into the former their ideas, the ideas of capitalism. Revisionism in the labour movement reflected these class pressures. The nearer a revolutionary situation, the more these ideological differences would be expressed in political and organizational differences. Hence the vital importance in a pre-revolutionary period of consciously combating revisionism. This theoretical fight is the anticipation of all the problems and divisions which the working class will have to overcome in its actual struggle for power.

The problem of proletarian class-consciousness is often discussed in a very abstract and general manner, instead of through the analysis of the actual historical process by which the Marxist movement and the working-class movement have developed. These are not two distinct processes: the conscious building of revolutionary parties is the highest form of the process by which the proletariat becomes a class 'for itself'. In the proper place, there is needed a critical analysis of all those writings on the working class and its consciousness which rely on concepts like 'affluence', 'prosperity', *'embourgeoisement'*, 'social mobility', and so on; and this analysis would have to deal with all the superficially very different and 'radical' approaches of writers like Marcuse. For the Marxist, such an analysis is of interest as an insight into the ideology of the bourgeoisie and petty bourgeoisie, reflecting their own historical situation and its changes, but it would at the same time be important in relation to the development of Marxism itself, because it bears directly on the most characteristic 'revision' of Marxism in our epoch: the rejection of the revolutionary role of the working class and of the need for revolutionary parties.

Class, for Marx, is rooted in social relations of production, and cannot be referred in the first place to relations of distribution and consumption or their ideological reflections. In considering the class-consciousness of the proletariat, Marxists are therefore not concerned with the ideas of individual workers about their position in society (no matter how many examples are collected and classified) so much as with the following series of categories: relations of production (sale of labour-power, exploitation); conflict of workers and employers on this basis (economic struggles, trade unions, elementary political battles for economic ends); conflict at the level of class (economic struggles which merge into the conflict between classes, which is organized through the political parties and the struggle for state power); the theoretical and practical struggle to build revolutionary parties of the working class, in conflict with non-revolutionary and counter-revolutionary tendencies in the class and their reflection inside the revolutionary party.

Thus, for example, a worker in the motor car industry will move through his elemental experience to an understanding of the gap between his own standard of life, income and conditions of work, on the one hand, and the mass of wealth to whose production he contributes, on the other. He will recognize an identity of interest, on this basis, with other wage-workers. 'Combinations' or trade unions are the adequate expression of this level of consciousness. To this 'trade union consciousness' may correspond other ideological, critical views on various aspects of capitalist society: for example, such consciousness can easily co-exist with that view which lays all the stress on differences or similarities in patterns of consumption; thus, elementary socialistic propaganda of the moralizing type, and modern pessimistic speculation about the workers' consciousness being dulled by the abundance of consumer goods, are types of consciousness which do not penetrate to the basis of class differences and class struggle and therefore cannot facilitate the development of political consciousness.

More 'sophisticated' socialist views of class-consciousness often refer to a process of more or less spontaneous political maturing through a series of economic struggles which take on greater and greater magnitude, finally posing demands which the system cannot meet. Here again the same basic error, from the Marxist standpoint, is made. In all such approaches, the class and its consciousness are seen in terms of a pre-Marxist theory of knowledge and of history. Those who put forward these ideas are unable to escape from a conception in which the separate *individuals* in the class move from their own working and other everyday experience to a higher level of consciousness, in this case political consciousness.

In point of fact an individual worker does not arrive through his own experience at a scientific consciousness of his actual relationship at work, let alone his political relationships. It is only when a worker comes into contact with the products, in political programme and action, of Marxist theory in politics — i.e., with the outcome of theoretical works produced in the first place by non-proletarians — that he can conceive of even his own working experience in terms which go beyond those of the prevailing bourgeois ideology. These works take the essence of the experience of the proletariat as well as all developments in economy, politics, science, the arts, etc.

Only a *historical* view of the working class and of the theory of Marxism, in their mutual interrelations, can produce a theory of *class*-consciousness. In the middle of the nineteenth century, Marx and Engels, working on various fields of learning, as well as analysing the experience of the struggle of the working class to that date, elaborated their theory of socialism. This theory is henceforth the essential component of the process by which the working class becomes a class 'for itself'. As a theory, it had first to penetrate beneath the day-to-day phenomenal forms of capitalist society to the social relations of production. It demonstrated that production under capitalism continues, and society develops, not through any conscious plan, but through the drive to produce surplus value, consequent upon the reduction of labour-power to a commodity, to units of 'abstract labour'. This is the essence of the worker's exploitation, rather than the fact, say, that he does not own the cars he produces. What he produces is essentially surplus value, the augmentation of that same capital which oppresses him.

From these basic relationships, Marx demonstrated the reality of the history of capitalism, the way in which private ownership came to a revolutionary clash with the further development of the forces of production. For a political or socialist consciousness of the struggle against the capitalist class, there is necessary the understanding of this historical tendency of the capitalist system. This means not just an abstract knowledge of the theory of historical materialism, but the concrete analysis of, and active engagement in, the development of the class struggle in all its forms and at all levels, in the period of capitalism's historical decline.

It was Lenin's major special contribution to Marxism to elaborate this theory of leadership and the revolutionary party, first of all in *What is to be Done?* and *One Step Forward, Two Steps Back*. But the whole of Lenin's work is an expression of this central concern. Later, Trotsky devoted a series of books and articles to the defence and development of the ideas worked out by Lenin (cf. particularly his *In Defence of Marxism* and *Lessons of October*, New Park Publications Ltd.). Gramsci also worked on important aspects of the relationship between Marxist theory and class consciousness, and developed further the critique of notions of spontaneity.

We have seen that even though the mass of workers experience capitalist exploitation, it is necessary for a struggle to take place between their existing consciousness, on the one hand, and Marxism on the other. This struggle is conducted, as part of the struggle of material forces, by the revolutionary Marxist party. The socialist revolution, like every social revolution, occupies an entire epoch. Its outcome is decided by a series of battles in every country, requiring the developed strategy and tactics of revolutionary parties and a revolutionary international whose whole outlook and experience is guided by the theoretical foundations laid by Marx.

Through the socialist revolution, men will enter 'the realm of freedom', says Marx. Consciousness will then not be the distorted ideology of oppressive social relations, resulting from the product's domination over the producer, but will be the expression of the scientifically-orientated will of the collective producers, of 'socialized humanity'. 'The free development of each will be the condition of the free development of all.'

Already the struggle of the working class against capitalism raises this fundamental question of the relation between subject and object, thus bringing Marx to say that philosophy can realize itself only through the proletariat. Capitalism poses the question in generalized from for the whole class in its relation to the rest of society, and thus demands nothing less than a revolutionary solution: '... the labour employed on the products appears here *as the value* of those products, as a material quality possessed by them.' (Marx, 'Critique of the Gotha Programme' in *Selected Works*, Vol. II, p. 563)

This 'reification', the value-form, in which a social relation between men in their most fundamental activity is transformed into a 'thing' standing outside and against men, is specific to the way in which the capitalist system continues the enslavement of man by man. This 'topsy-turvy world' becomes in sociology a world of 'social facts', of 'roles', faithfully recorded as the necessary framework of experience.

Just as the working class in its struggle must reject this split between subject and object as a threat to its very humanity, so must Marxist theory penetrate beneath it and point the way to its internal contradictions and historical fate. The real relation between the working class and its product is obscured in the first place by the fact that the labour appears to have been paid for in wages, and that there the matter ends. Marx says that this illusion of wages as the proper reward for labour is the key to all the ideology of capitalism (*Capital*, Vol. I, p. 550). Marx exploded this illusion in theory, and thus opened the path for its being exploded in practice. That path leads from trade union consciousness (a fair day's pay for a fair day's work!) to socialist consciousness.

Working-class consciousness is then, for Marxists, the comprehending in struggle of the process through which the proletariat develops from its identity as formed by capitalism (the mass of exploited wage-labourers, the class 'in itself') to the working class organized as a revolutionary force for the taking of power and the building of socialism (the class 'for itself'). This process must be grasped *dialectically*, i.e., as a conflict of opposites, a real conflict between the class as it is and as the Marxist movement fights for it to be, on the basis of analysing the objective developments in society. It is the failure to recognize and to begin from this conflict which restricts, for example, the work of Lukacs in his *History and Class Consciousness* (1923-1924). Lukacs cannot get beyond the concept of 'adjudged' or 'adequate' consciousness, which is abstracted by the investigator according to his scientific estimation of the needs of the class historically. This remains at the level of the type of concepts developed by bourgeois sociology (particularly Max Weber), and fails to reach the level of dialectical materialism, at the centre of which is the unity of theory and practice as a contradictory process. Lukacs' own subsequent capitulation to Stalinism, whatever other causes it had, was rooted in this static and essentially idealist conception of class-consciousness, imported from neo-Kantian philosophy. It helped him in a very crude way to accept and become an apologist for Stalinist orthodoxy in the communist movement.

Lukacs asserted that the central concept of dialectics is 'totality'; and here again he shows the inadequacy of his outlook for a theory of class-consciousness. For Marx, the struggle, the unity and the interpenetration of opposites is the essence of dialectics, and this dialectic is materialist, so that for Marxists the notion of totality must have a meaning different from that presented by Lukacs. 'The unity of the world consists in its materiality,' wrote Engels. It is characteristic of Lukacs' agnosticism on the question of the objective nature of the external world (in *History and Class Consciousness*) that he must take 'totality' and the proletariat's grasp of this totality as an abstraction. Only a view of the 'unity' or 'totality' of the objective world of nature and society which sees this unity as arising continuously from a changing conflict of material opposites can form the basis of 'revolutionary practice', the *sine qua non* of Marx's theory of knowledge.

Henri Lefèbvre (in his *The Sociology of Marx*, Allen Lane, the Penguin Press, 1968, and elsewhere) has criticized Lukacs for his stress on 'totality' and has argued that 'the conflict of opposites' is in fact the core of dialectics. However, in Lefèbvre's work this correct criticism remains purely abstract, and leads him eventually to Utopianism. He starts from the concept of a struggle of opposites, but leaves it at the level of the very *general* concepts of *praxis* and *alienation*. These terms, taken from Marx's early work, enable Lefèbvre to make often penetrating exposés of capitalist culture, but they remain altogether too abstract for a revolutionary theory of class-consciousness. The theory remains purely critical, aloof from practice, i.e., from the activity of the class and the fight for a working-class leadership on a Marxist basis.

Lefèbvre criticizes, for example, Lucien Goldmann, because the latter, developing the work of Lukacs, over-emphasizes the phenomenon of 'reification' so much that his argument amounts to a virtual acceptance, rather than a criticism, of the forms of objectivity imposed on consciousness by capitalist society. But this criticism is inadequate, and needs in the end to be turned against Lefèbvre himself. Goldmann in the period between 1957 and his death in 1973, expressed complete scepticism about the revolutionary role of the working class under modern capitalism. He did so on the grounds that, besides certain economic and political changes in the capitalist system, such as the part played by state intervention in the economy, the ability of capitalism to supply an ever-increasing amount of consumer goods had eroded working-class consciousness. This suggests immediately that Goldmann's original reasons for accepting the revolutionary character of the proletariat were unsound, from the Marxist standpoint (see his articles in *Les Temps Modernes* for 1957 and 1958, reprinted in *Recherches Dialectiques*, Paris, 1959). Goldmann conceives of ideas and ideologies as mental translations of economic and social patterns, rather than as the outcome of the struggles of the class at all levels of social reality (see chapter VI above), and this has provided an avenue for him to accept the fashionable 'structuralist' school of idealism in France.

The actual contradictory process of the struggle for revolutionary consciousness, the conflicts between theory and practice, between party and class and, concretely, the struggle of tendencies within the labour movement and within the revolutionary party, and the class bases of these struggles — all these are almost completely lacking in any of the often interesting commentaries of these writers, whose works appeal so much to those who look for some pure or 'restored' Marxism, rediscovered by removing all the results of a century and more of bitter struggle as the theory has taken on flesh and blood. The 'young Marx' is the usual gospel of this faith. It would be in the spirit of Marx himself to aim for a Marxism which is rich and concrete, and at the same time warlike, having worked over and 'negated' all the contradictory developments in the proletarian revolution, and above all in the communist movement itself. For the various 'schools' of Marxism in France and their faint echoes outside, the issue is indeed presented much more concretely than they would like: to really develop the Marxist method and concepts for the analysis of modern capitalist society and of the USSR, it is necessary to start from a conscious reintegration with the whole actual past struggle for Marxism against the social democrats and then the Stalinists and revisionists who distorted it. That means an identification with the continuity of the fight for Marxism of Lenin and Trotsky, and in particular against the Stalinist domination of working-class politics and of 'Marxism' in France.

In the most fundamental theoretical terms, Lefèbvre has missed out what was potentially correct in Lukacs' insistence on 'totality': the struggle of opposites in society must be taken as first and foremost a *class* conflict, *at the level of the social whole*. To analyse, and to start in all social analyses from this, requires of course a concentration on the *specific* contradictions of capitalism and of the development of the working class and its revolutionary consciousness within capitalism. Marx himself developed his ideas from the general notions of *praxis* and *alienation* of humanity in his early works to the specific analysis of the historically developing social relations of capitalism, out of which grew all the 'praxis' and 'alienation' of modern man. By returning to the early Marx for the key to capitalist society today, Lefèbvre opens the door to a reformist and Utopian critique of culture, instead of a consistent and revolutionary theory and practice, in conflict with the

Stalinist distortion of Marxism in every field. His works *Critique de la Vie Quotidienne* (Vol II, 1960, Editions de L'Arche) and *Introduction à la Modernité* (Editions de Minuit, 1962) reveal this tendency very clearly: a searching for a 'poetic' quality in particular aspects of life, a contrast between creative and repetitive actions which is made a more general and important distinction than the specific historical contradictions of capitalism and the tasks of revolutionary transformation which they pose to the working class and to Marxists.

Our argument here does not simplify the question of class-consciousness. On the contrary, it opens up a prospect which cannot be settled purely by words. Theory must become conscious of its real relationship with its subject-matter, and consciously guide the revolutionary struggle to transform it. This is the essence of dialectical materialism in Marx's work. For the working class to become a class 'for itself' requires not simply the absorption of the experience of capitalist society, but the critical struggle against this experience by a party armed with the whole theory of Marxism. Party and class are two interpenetrating opposites at one level (the class 'for itself' and the class 'in itself'). These two poles at the same time constitute a whole (the working class) which itself is one pole as against its opposite (the capitalist class) in another contradictory whole (capitalist society). Society confronts nature as its 'opposite'. The working class must realize itself, against capitalism, subsuming all the historical gains for humanity made by capitalism at the same time as overthrowing it. This it can do only when the outlook, strategy and tactics of a Marxist party predominate in the actions of the class as a class, in revolutionary struggles. A similar process is necessary within the party: only if it can study, unify and transform through struggle all the experiences of the class can its theory be saved from one-sidedness, dogma and idealism. Within the Marxist party, once again we have a struggle of opposites, a struggle for the development of Marxist theory and its application to the struggles of the proletariat, in constant struggle against every mode of adaptation to the existing position of the working class, its disunity, fragmentation, etc., those aspects of its situation which predispose it towards acceptance of its oppression. Then theory itself must also be considered as a struggle of opposites. We have seen that at every level, each pole of a unity of opposites contains a recapitulation of the total opposition within itself (e.g. the party has both its own essence and its opposite *within* it and not only as an external opposite, etc.). Marxist theory develops by proving the 'concreteness' of its abstractions against the apparent concreteness (really abstractness, because abstracted from the changing forces which produce them) of uncritically accepted empirical reality. It does this through a struggle to change that reality, capitalism, by placing itself politically in a relation of political consciousness, leadership, with the working class. That means the struggle to build revolutionary parties able to lead the working class to power. Marxism is this struggle: it is not a sociology or an abstract theoretical system of any kind.

Select bibliography

1843	Marx: Critique of Hegel's Philosophy of Right (Cambridge, 1970)
1844	Marx: Introduction to the Critique of Hegel's Philosophy of Right (in Marx and Engels, *On Religion*, Moscow 1957)
1844	Marx: Economic and Philosophical Manuscripts (Lawrence and Wishart, 1970)
1844	Marx and Engels: The Holy Family (Moscow, 1964)
1845	Marx: Theses on Feuerbach (Marx-Engels *Selected Works*, Lawrence and Wishart, 1970)
1846	Marx and Engels: The German Ideology (Moscow, 1965. Some sections only, Lawrence and Wishart, 1970)
1847	Marx: The Poverty of Philosophy (Moscow)
1847	Marx and Engels: The Communist Manifesto (Marx-Engels *Selected Works*, Lawrence and Wishart, 1970)
1850	Marx: The Class Struggles in France (*Revolutions of 1848*, Penguin Books, 1974)
1851	Marx: Address to the Communist League (*Revolutions of 1848*, Penguin Books, 1974)
1852	Marx: The Eighteenth Brumaire of Louis Bonaparte (Marx-Engels *Selected Works*, Lawrence and Wishart, 1970)
1857-59	Marx: Foundations of a Critique of Political Economy (*Grundrisse*) (Penguin Books, 1973)
1859	Marx: Contribution to the Critique of Political Economy (Moscow 1971)
1862	Marx: Theories of Surplus Value (Lawrence and Wishart 1969-71)
1863-77	Capital, Volumes I, II, III (Lawrence and Wishart, 1954-59)
1871	The Civil War in France (Marx-Engels *Selected Works*, Lawrence and Wishart 1970)
1875	Marx: Critique of the Gotha Programme (Marx-Engels *Selected Works*, Lawrence and Wishart 1970)
	Marx and Engels: Selected Correspondence (Moscow, 1965)

Year	
1878	Engels: Anti-Duhring (Moscow, 1959)
1884	Engels: The Origin of the Family, Private Property and the State (Marx-Engels *Selected Works*, Lawrence and Wishart, 1970)
1888	Engels: Ludwig Feuerbach (Marx-Engels *Selected Works*, Lawrence and Wishart, 1970)
1894	Lenin: What the 'Friends of the People' Are and How They Help the Social Democrats (*Collected Works*, Moscow, Volume 1)
1902	Lenin: What is to be Done? (Volume 5)
1903	Lenin: One Step Forward, Two Steps Back (Volume 7)
1913	The Three Sources and Three Component Parts of Marxism (Volume 19)
1915	Lenin: Philosophical Notebooks (Volume 38)
1917	Lenin: The State and Revolution (Volume 25)
1918	Lenin: The Proletarian Revolution and the Renegade Kautsky (Volume 28)
1925	Trotsky: Where is Britain Going? (*Collected Writings and Speeches on Britain*, Volume 2, New Park Publications, 1975)
1930	Trotsky: Permanent Revolution (New Park Publications, 1971)
1930-32	Trotsky: History of the Russian Revolution (Sphere Books, 1967)
1934	Trotsky: The Class Nature of the Soviet State (New Park Publications, 1973)
1936	Trotsky: Whither France? (New Park Publications, 1974)
1940	Trotsky: In Defence of Marxism (New Park Publications, 1971)